The Lean Leader

Promote efficiency. Improve Joy at work. Empower your team. Remove waste. Lead with Lean.

Michael Bayer

KAIZEN
FORGE PRESS

Copyright © 2025 by Kaizen Forge Press

All rights reserved.

No portion of this book may be reproduced in any form without written permission from the publisher or author, except as permitted by U.S. copyright law.

For my Daughters

This book is about leading with clarity. With purpose. With respect for people and the work they do every day. That is what I hope to pass on. Not just to the teams I support. But to you.

You will not need a title to lead. You will not need permission to make something better. You will only need to stay close to what is real. To listen. To act. To show up with honesty and discipline when it matters most.

That is what I wanted this book to capture. Not theory. Behavior. Not a system. A way of thinking. I wrote it to help others find their voice in the noise. But mostly, I wrote it to leave something behind for you.

If you ever wonder what your dad believed in, what he stood for, it is all here. In every page. In every line.

Work with purpose. Lead with respect. Make things better.

That is the job. That is the gift.

And that is what I see in you every day.

Author's Welcome

Welcome, and thank you for stepping into the world of leading with Lean. I appreciate your decision to begin this work. With nearly two decades of experience as a Lean Six Sigma consultant and coach, I have partnered with many leaders facing real organizational challenges. The tools and insights we will explore are grounded in experience and have been applied successfully in many environments.

This journey is not about trends or theory. It is about learning to think differently, lead with intention, and improve what matters. We will focus on strategies that reduce waste, increase efficiency, and create a workplace where people are empowered to do their best work. These ideas are practical, repeatable, and designed to deliver results.

Leading with Lean requires more than skill. It requires honesty, persistence, and a willingness to challenge the way things have always been done. This process will push you. It should. Growth requires discomfort, and progress requires change.

My goal is simple. I want to provide something useful. If this book prompts reflection, creates clarity, or helps you take action, then it has served its purpose. I believe better is always possible and that good leaders, equipped with the right mindset and tools, can transform their teams and organizations.

Let's get started.

Chapter One

The Lean Leadership Paradigm

Lean did not start in a boardroom. It started because work was not working. People were stuck. Processes were messy. Time was wasted. The only way forward was to stop tolerating the clutter and start fixing what was in the way.

That is still true.

Most teams are not short on effort. They are short on clarity. Work moves, but no one is sure where it lands. Problems get patched, not solved. Communication is scattered. Leaders know something is off, but they do not always know where to begin. That is where Lean fits. Not as a framework. Not as a toolkit. As a way to lead when the work is harder than it needs to be.

This is not about history. It is not about Toyota. It is about now. What Lean did in a factory decades ago is interesting. But what matters more is what it can do for the person waiting on a system response, reworking a customer issue, or wondering why their team is always behind. That is the moment Lean becomes real. When it is about your work. Not someone else's. Not a theory. Just a better way to lead what is right in front of you.

The tools came later. The mindset came first. See the problem. Remove the waste. Fix what blocks the team. That is the foundation. And that is what this book will help you do. Not by following steps. By solving what actually matters.

Let's get into it.

Moving on from Toyota

We ***do not mention Toyota*** when teaching or applying Lean in transactional businesses because the context is too far removed from what these teams experience. While Toyota is foundational to Lean's history, bringing it up in service sectors often creates more confusion than clarity. The environments are different, the problems are different, and the people doing the work do not see the connection. When someone working in a hospital, a bank, or a software company hears about car manufacturing, they immediately tune out. The comparison does not feel relevant. The tools may have originated there, but the application has to feel local to be accepted.

Referencing Toyota can unintentionally send the message that Lean is meant for production lines, not knowledge work. That perception creates a barrier. In addition, many transactional teams have already encountered Lean in the form of failed rollouts or surface-level training that focused too much on manufacturing examples. For these teams, Lean already feels misaligned. Mentioning Toyota reinforces the idea that Lean is for someone else, not for them. If you bought a round of *The Machine that Changed the World* or the equally popular, albeit unrelated to American transactional businesses, *The Toyota Way* for your team, you have already lost an important first battle: making the methodology relevant to them.

Instead, we use examples that reflect their reality. We talk about delays in patient care, backlogs in processing, or perhaps friction in customer service. We connect Lean to the work they know, using their language. Once the principles are grounded in their environment, the value becomes clear. They do not need to know where it started. They need to see that it works here. Toyota belongs in the history of Lean, not in the front of the room when teaching transactional teams. The moment Lean becomes about their work, not someone else's, is the moment they start to listen. That is when the shift begins.

Introducing Lean Sans Toyota

A better way for a leader to introduce Lean in a transactional setting is to start with the problems the team already experiences and wants to fix. The leader does not need to reference the past or another industry. Credibility comes from showing that Lean addresses the exact issues that make work harder than it needs to be.

Begin by naming what is already true. Processes are unclear. Work sits in queues. People spend too much time correcting mistakes or chasing updates. These are not dramatic failures. They are daily pain points. By calling them out, the leader signals that improvement is possible and that the current state is not something the team has to accept. The next step is to position Lean as a way to make work easier and more consistent. This is not about theory. It is about making sure the right work gets done with less friction. It is not a new program or a temporary fix. It is a practical approach to improve how teams operate. When presented this way, Lean does not feel abstract. It feels like common sense.

The leader also builds trust by being clear about what Lean will not become. It is not a way to cut headcount. It is not a scoreboard. It is not about doing more with less. It is about doing the right work in the right way and letting the people closest to the work lead the changes. This clarity removes suspicion and helps teams stay engaged. One of the strongest ways to give Lean credibility is to use real examples from inside the organization. If a team improved a workflow and reduced delays, tell that story. If a simple change saved time or improved service, share the result. These examples do not need to be perfect. They need to be real. People believe what they see. Most importantly, the leader must model the behavior they expect. They ask questions instead of making assumptions. They support experiments even when the outcome is not perfect. They create space for others to improve their own work. This is what gives Lean staying power. When people see that the leader is consistent, Lean becomes part of the culture, not just another project. This approach works because it is built on relevance, trust, and action. It makes Lean about solving real problems in real time, and that is where it belongs.

The Five Step Introduction to Lean

Step 1: Start with the problem

When introducing Lean, you do not begin with a definition or a tool. You start by focusing on what is broken. That means talking about the work, not the theory. You begin with what slows people down, what causes rework, and what leads to unnecessary steps. Your team may not know what Lean is, but they know what gets in their way. This is not about launching an initiative, it is about helping people fix what already frustrates them. Ask the team what makes their job harder than it needs to be. Let them speak without framing their answers. You are not gathering input for a business case. You are showing that their experience matters and that solving those problems is the point. That is what earns trust and gets people to listen. If Lean is introduced as a solution to a problem the team actually feels, they are more likely to support it. If it is presented as a program looking for something to fix, it will be ignored. Start with the problem because that is where change begins. It proves that Lean is not about checking boxes, it is about making the work better.

Step 2: Define what Lean is and is not

Once the team sees that you are serious about solving real problems, the next step is to make sure everyone understands what Lean actually means. You do not need a perfect definition. You need a simple explanation that connects to their work. Lean is a way to make work clearer, faster, and less frustrating. It helps teams focus on what matters by removing what gets in the way. That is it. Keep it that direct. Avoid overexplaining or turning it into a history lesson. This is not the time for frameworks or labels. It is the time to make Lean feel useful.

At the same time, you need to be clear about what Lean is not. It is not about cutting headcount. It is not a management trend. It is not about going faster for the sake of speed. It is not a one time fix. This matters because most people have seen tools rolled out before with good intentions but poor results. They are used to change being something that is done to them, not with them. If you are not clear about what Lean is and what it is not, people will assume it is another version of the same thing they have seen fail. Credibility comes from clarity. When you introduce Lean as a way to improve the work, not manage the people, you give it room to take hold. When you tell the truth about what it is and how it will be used, you give your team a reason to trust you. That trust is the foundation for everything that comes next.

Step 3: Find an early win

After the team understands what Lean is and feels that it is grounded in their reality, the next step is to make it real. That means finding a problem that can be solved quickly and visibly. Not the most complicated issue. Not the biggest opportunity. Just something specific, annoying, and fixable. Look for delays, bottlenecks, or unclear handoffs. Look for anything that wastes time or creates extra steps. The point is to pick something small enough to solve and important enough that people will care if it gets better.

Once you have that problem, solve it with the team. Use a basic visual board, walk the process, or ask the five whys. Do not overdesign the solution. Do not turn it into a project. Stay focused on getting to a better outcome with the least amount of effort. When the change works, show what improved. Was it faster? Clearer? Did it reduce rework or eliminate confusion? The outcome does not need to be dramatic. It just needs to be real. The purpose of the early win is not to prove Lean works. It is to show the team that they can improve their own work and that leadership will support them when they do. That shift in belief is what moves Lean from something new to something valuable. People trust what they experience. A well chosen early win builds that trust. It turns ideas into action and creates momentum you can build on.

Step 4: Share the story

Once the early win is in place, the next step is to make sure people hear about it. Not through a presentation. Not through metrics. Through a simple, clear story about what changed and why it mattered. Keep the focus on the team. What problem did they solve? What did they do differently? What got better because of it? The more direct the story, the more believable it becomes. This is not about promoting Lean. It is about showing people what improvement looks like when it is done by the people doing the work.

When you share the story, do it in a way that feels familiar. Use the team's language. Talk about the process they fixed. Explain what made the change possible. Keep it short. Avoid trying to make it sound like a breakthrough. The point is to normalize improvement, not glorify it. People do not need to be impressed. They need to see that change is possible in their space, with their tools, and within their control. The story becomes the example others will point to. It becomes the reason someone else takes a first step. When they hear that a real team made something better without waiting for permission or a new system, it gives them permission to try. That is how Lean spreads. One simple story at a time. Not by strategy, but by proof.

Step 5: Lead through action

At this point, the team has seen what Lean can do. They have solved a problem, shared the outcome, and started to shift how they think about improvement. Now they are watching you. What you do next will decide whether Lean becomes part of how the organization works or just another short term effort that fades out. This step is not about managing the rollout. It is about leading in a way that reflects the principles you are asking others to follow.

Ask better questions. Do not just ask for status updates. Ask what is getting in the way and what has been improved this week. Support problem solving even when the results are not perfect. Make it clear that progress is more valuable than perfection. Remove blockers when they show up. If the team needs access to data, a faster decision, or help from another group, your job is to clear the path. This is how you show that improvement is not just encouraged. It is expected. Be consistent. Do not talk about Lean and then act in a way that contradicts it. If you ask for feedback, respond to it. If you say something is important, make time for it. Your actions define the culture more than any statement or training. When people see that you are willing to change how you lead, they are more likely to change how they work. This is where Lean either takes root or stops growing. If it becomes something leaders do, it becomes something others do too. Not because they were told, but because it makes sense. That is how Lean becomes the way work gets done. Not through words. Through action.

Back in my day. An author reflection.

Back in my day, I watched Lean get rolled out at a large financial institution in a way that still makes me cringe. It had all the markings of a textbook implementation, but none of the discipline or context needed to make it work. The organization had invested heavily. Leaders were all in. They hired consultants, built a branded training program, and launched a series of mandatory workshops that opened with the Toyota Production System as their North Star. Slide after slide showed car parts, factory floors, and assembly line metrics. The message was clear. If it worked for Toyota, it should work for us.

Except it didn't.

The people actually doing the work, subject matter experts who ran complex financial processes every day, were not impressed. They could not see themselves in the training. Nothing about their work resembled a factory. The tools felt forced. The examples felt recycled. When they asked questions, they were met with more manufacturing analogies. That was the beginning of the divide. Leaders were sold. Frontline teams were not. The consultants kept pushing ahead, confident in the process. But nothing stuck.

Meetings were held. Workgroups were formed. Tools were introduced. Nobody believed any of it. The teams treated it like another initiative they needed to survive or outlive. Improvement projects were filled with templates and buzzwords but lacked clarity or urgency. Nobody asked what problems actually needed to be solved. They just followed the steps and filled in the blanks. It looked structured from the outside, but inside it was a soup sandwich. Messy, hard to hold together, and no one wanted to eat it.

Eventually, the effort lost steam. The branding faded. The posters came down. Some of the language stuck, but the meaning never landed. It failed not because people were resistant, but because the approach skipped the one thing that makes Lean work. It never started with their problems. It started with Toyota's.

In Summary

Introducing Lean the right way is not about programs, presentations, or polished definitions. It is about anchoring Lean in the daily work, solving problems that matter, and doing it in a way that feels useful and believable. When Lean is introduced through clarity, relevance, and action, it becomes a tool for the team, not just a priority for leadership. The shift happens when people see that Lean is not an external solution but a method to make their own work better. That is how momentum builds. That is how change lasts.

Now that we have covered how to introduce Lean with intention, the next step is to explore why it matters in the long run. At its core, Lean is about creating value and removing what does not. When applied well, this shift does more than improve flow or simplify steps. It produces measurable cost savings without taking away from the customer or the team. In the next chapter, we will look closely at how Lean creates cost efficiency and what it takes to achieve it without damaging trust, speed, or quality.

Chapter Two

Cost Efficiency through Lean

Let's be honest. Most leaders do not adopt Lean because they wake up one day wanting better flow or smoother processes. They adopt Lean because they need results. Cost efficiency is almost always part of the conversation. It is the driver that gets leadership to take action. We talk about customer experience, and that absolutely matters, but the truth is that no organization invests in Lean unless there is a clear financial incentive to do so.

That does not make it wrong. It makes it real. Leaders are accountable for budgets. They are expected to do more with the same or sometimes less. When Lean is positioned as a way to reduce cost without hurting the customer or the team, it starts to make sense. But that only happens when it is done the right way. Lean is not about cutting for the sake of cutting. It is about removing waste that adds no value so that resources can be spent where they matter most.

This chapter focuses on how Lean creates cost efficiency without damaging the very things the business depends on: its people, its quality, and its ability to serve. We will walk through how to identify the right cost opportunities, how to track the impact, and how to build a financial case that earns support without losing trust. If you want Lean to stick, it has to prove its worth. This is how you do it.

Creating cost efficiency through Lean starts with identifying the right opportunities. Not every cost is waste, and not every expense should be reduced. Chasing savings without context leads to short-term cuts that hurt long-term performance. The goal is not to shrink the budget. The goal is to spend smarter by removing what adds no value and reinvesting in what does. This requires discipline, focus, and a practical use of Lean tools.

You start with the customer. Not because it sounds good, but because value is defined by the customer, not by the organization. The first question is simple. What are we doing that the customer actually cares about? This question anchors the entire exercise. If a task, process, or requirement does not directly contribute to delivering that value, it becomes a candidate for closer inspection. It might be necessary. It might be required. But it is not value added. That distinction matters.

The best way to see this clearly is through **value stream mapping**. This is not a swim lane diagram or a process flow. It is a structured look at how work moves from start to finish for a given product, service, or transaction. You map every step. You capture the handoffs, the queues, the delays, and the rework. But more importantly, you label each activity as value added, non-value added but necessary, or pure waste. This visual separates what is essential from what has simply become normal.

Excuse me, but what is a value stream map?

Great question, I am glad you asked! A value stream map shows the full sequence of activities needed to deliver a product or service, but what sets it apart is its ability to expose how work crosses boundaries. It is not limited to what one team sees. It connects departments, roles, and systems so you can trace the full journey of the work. It also includes symbols to show where decisions happen, where approvals are required, and where information flows in or out. In transactional settings, this often reveals that the biggest delays are not in the steps themselves but in the handoffs between them. This tool helps uncover those gaps so they can be addressed directly.

As you build the value stream map, focus on time and flow. Use **process cycle efficiency** to see the percentage of time that is actually spent on value added activity. If you are spending three days to do ten minutes of meaningful work, that is a cost opportunity. Use **takt time** to understand the pace at which work needs to be completed to meet demand. If you are building inventory that no one asked for, or if your resources are idle waiting on upstream steps, those are signs of imbalance that increase cost.

Excuse me, but what is process cycle efficiency?

Another great question! Process cycle efficiency, or PCE for short, is a way to measure how much of the total time spent in a process is actually used to create value. It answers a simple question: of all the time it takes to complete the work, how much is spent doing something the customer would care about?

You calculate it by dividing the total value added time by the total lead time, then express it as a percentage. Value added time is the hands-on work that moves the product or service forward. Lead time includes everything, including waiting, delays, handoffs, and rework. A low percentage means most of the time is spent on things that do not add value. A higher percentage means the process is efficient and focused. This measure helps you separate activity from progress. It shows how much of the total time is productive versus how much is just motion. It also gives you a simple baseline to improve from. The higher the PCE, the more efficient the process.

Ok, great. What about takt time?

You are really getting good at asking the right questions! Takt time is the rate at which a product or service needs to be completed to meet customer demand. It gives you a simple way to align the pace of your process with the pace of what is actually needed. You calculate it by dividing the available working time by the customer demand during that same time period. Takt time is not how fast you can work. It is how fast you should work to stay balanced with demand. If your actual process time is longer than your takt time, you will fall behind. If it is much shorter, you may be overproducing or wasting resources. In a transactional setting, it helps teams avoid overloading one part of the system while others sit idle.

This measure helps set the rhythm for consistent, sustainable output. It keeps the focus on flow instead of speed. Matching the work to takt time prevents bottlenecks and highlights where adjustments are needed to stay on pace without burning out the team or overbuilding what is not needed. Don't worry, we address this in more detail in a later chapter!

Look closely at rework. Use a **pareto chart** to find the most common failure points. Ask why they happen. Use the five whys or other root cause analysis tools to move past surface-level answers. Rework is a quiet cost. It consumes time, people, and materials, often without showing up on a budget line. Eliminating the need for it is one of the fastest ways to recover cost without cutting anything visible to the customer.

Excuse me, but what is a Pareto Chart?

Four for four with questions this chapter! A Pareto chart shows where the biggest problems are. It arranges the issues from most frequent to least, so you can see which ones are doing the most damage. The idea is simple. Most of your problems come from a few sources. You do not need to fix everything. You need to fix the right things. This chart helps you see that clearly. If you are tracking customer complaints, defects, or delays, the Pareto chart tells you which ones to start with. You spend your time where it matters most and stop wasting energy on issues that do not move the needle. The bars show the size of the issue. The line shows the cumulative impact. You can see where the drop off happens and know exactly when to stop chasing small problems. The idea comes from the Pareto principle, which suggests that a small number of causes are responsible for the majority of the problems. You often hear it called the 80-20 rule where roughly 80 percent of effects come from 20 percent of the causes.

This tool keeps teams focused. It keeps improvement efforts from being scattered or driven by opinion. It is not about the number of items. It is about the impact. And that is what Lean is meant to deliver. More to come in a later chapter on Pareto Charts.

Next, examine handoffs and approvals. These are usually hidden pockets of delay and inefficiency. Use **spaghetti diagrams** if you are in a physical space or **process observation** if the work is digital. Watch what really happens. How many times does something change hands? How long does it sit in queues? How many touchpoints add no value? Every time something waits, moves, or requires a signoff with no clear purpose, there is cost being added with no value in return.

A spaghetti what?!

I know, the tool title makes you hungry. Me as well. A spaghetti diagram shows how work moves through a physical space. You track the actual path a person or product takes to complete a task. The lines look like a mess, which is where the name comes from. The more tangled the lines, the more waste you are likely to find. This tool helps you see unnecessary motion, backtracking, and poor layout. It gives you a visual way to spot inefficiencies that slow people down without relying on assumptions. You can then redesign the space to shorten the distance, reduce movement, and make the work easier to complete.

What about process observation?

Process observation is exactly what it sounds like. You watch the work as it happens. You are not reviewing reports or relying on what people think is happening. You are seeing it yourself. This tool is useful when the work is digital or service based and cannot be mapped through physical movement. You watch how tasks are triggered, how long they wait, and what causes delays. You document what actually happens, not what should happen. It gives you real insight into where time is lost, where confusion exists, and where handoffs break down. You are not there to audit. You are there to learn.

Do not overlook meetings, reports, and metrics. These are often justified in the name of communication or oversight, but if they are not being used to make decisions, they are waste. Conduct a **time study** or **activity sampling** to quantify how much time is spent on administrative work that does not move the process forward. The numbers are usually worse than expected. The cost is real, and it comes in the form of lost capacity and buried frustration.

A time study? At work?!

Yes! A time 'study' measures how long each part of a task actually takes. You break the work into steps and track the time for each one. This helps you see where time is well spent and where it is wasted. It also makes it clear which steps vary the most from person to person. That variation is usually where the problems start. A time study gives you the facts you need to set a baseline, spot inefficiencies, and make better decisions about staffing, flow, or standard work.

A sample through observation? Really?!

Yes, and it needs to be reflective! Activity sampling takes a broader view. Instead of tracking one person from start to finish, you take snapshots of what people are doing at random intervals. Over time, the data shows how work time is really spent across a team or function. You learn how much time goes to value added work, how much goes to support tasks, and how much is lost in waiting or motion. This tool is useful when direct observation is not practical over a long period. It helps you see patterns, not just isolated issues, and gives you a high level picture of where the time actually goes.

Once you have identified areas of waste, focus on quantifying the opportunity. Use **cost of poor quality** to calculate the real expense of defects, delays, and complaints. Include the cost of rework, additional labor, lost customers, and recovery efforts. Then use standard work to define what good looks like and measure the gap between current and ideal. That difference is your opportunity.

What about the cost of poor quality?

Cost of poor quality is the total expense a business pays for work that was not done right the first time. That includes defects, delays, rework, complaints, missed deadlines, and anything else that forces the team to spend extra time fixing what should have already been finished. It also includes what is lost: customer trust, follow-up opportunities, and reputation. These costs rarely show up in one place. They are scattered across budgets and buried in daily work. That makes them easy to ignore and hard to defend unless you measure them.

You break the cost into categories. Internal failures are caught before they reach the customer. External failures are caught after. Both require time, effort, and often money to correct. You also track appraisal costs, like inspections or audits, and prevention costs, like training or standard work. The point is to shift resources from fixing problems to preventing them. If you do not track this, improvement sounds optional. When you do track it, the case for change becomes obvious. It stops being about process and starts being about money.

Now that you have the data, you shift to prioritization. Do not chase every savings idea. Start with what is big, visible, and controllable. Use an **impact versus effort matrix** to rank the opportunities. Look for actions that can be implemented quickly with a strong return. Build credibility early by showing results that matter. Use kaizen events, renamed to fit your organization, to drive focused, fast-paced improvements with cross-functional teams. These events bring visibility, align decision makers, and create energy that builds momentum.

What's this Impact versus effort matrix, now?

An impact versus effort matrix helps you decide what is worth doing first. You take your list of improvements and sort them by how much effort they require and how much impact they create. The goal is to identify changes that will deliver results quickly without pulling too many resources. High impact with low effort goes to the top. Low impact with high effort falls off the list.

This tool keeps teams focused. It prevents wasted time on low value work and stops ideas from gaining traction just because someone likes them. It gives leaders a clear way to prioritize without emotion. When used consistently, it helps drive results without losing momentum or overloading the team.

Throughout this process, stay close to the team. Lean does not work from a spreadsheet. It works when the people closest to the work are involved in diagnosing and improving it. Use their knowledge to validate what the data says. Let them tell you what adds value and what gets in their way. This not only produces better insights. It also builds ownership. When teams help identify the opportunity, they are far more likely to support the change.

To sum it up, the right cost opportunities are not just the biggest numbers. They are the activities that add no value, slow things down, or create frustration. You identify them by mapping the work, measuring the flow, and engaging the people who know the process best. The right Lean tools make the invisible visible and give you the clarity needed to improve without guessing. Cost efficiency starts with understanding where waste lives and having the discipline to fix it without cutting what matters. That is the Lean approach. Simple, focused, and rooted in reality.

Proving the efficiency

> Identifying waste is not enough. At some point, you have to translate it into something leadership cannot ignore. That means speaking their language. You move from activity to outcome. You move from insight to value. If you want Lean to keep going, it has to earn the right to stay. You do that by showing how it improves the bottom line without asking people to work harder or accept less.

This section will cover how to build that case. Not with complicated models, but with clear connections. We will walk through how to calculate savings without overselling. How to show benefits beyond cost alone. And how to present the results in a way that builds trust and secures more support. Lean does not just cut cost. It creates capacity, improves quality, and strengthens service. But if you cannot show that clearly, the work risks being seen as effort without return.

Let's move into how to make the value visible so that Lean gets the investment it deserves.

Step 1: Quantify what changed

If you want Lean to be taken seriously, you start by being precise. Do not say the process got better. Say exactly what changed. Did the cycle time drop? Did the number of touchpoints go down? Did fewer items get kicked back for correction? If you cannot name it, you cannot measure it. And if you cannot measure it, leadership will not fund it. You do not need a full dashboard or a system overhaul. You need to show that something that mattered was improved. That might be the time it takes to complete a task, the number of people required to do it, or the volume of work completed in a given period. Look at before and after. Compare the actual numbers. How long did it take then? How long does it take now? What was the error rate before? What is it today? Be direct. Use facts. Strip away the noise.

If the team eliminated steps, count them. If they removed rework loops, name them. If they reduced handoffs, show the difference. This is not about overexplaining. It is about showing the change in a way that anyone can see. That clarity builds confidence.

You also need to make sure you are not overstating the improvement. The goal is not to impress. The goal is to prove that Lean works. When you stay grounded in actual results, it builds credibility. That credibility is the foundation for the rest of the business case. If you skip this step, everything that follows starts to sound like a pitch. Quantify the change. Make it real. Then move on to what it means.

1. Start with a clear before and after comparison. Pick one thing that the improvement was meant to affect. Was it time? Volume? Accuracy? Rework? Make sure you have the number from before the change and the number from after. Do not guess. If you do not have the old data, start collecting now so you can track it for the next one.

2. Use manual tracking if systems are slow. Watch the work. Count how long it takes or how many steps it goes through. Sit with the team and mark down how many files are touched, how long they wait, or how often they get sent back. You do not need software to see waste. You need a clipboard and a chair.

3. Track results with simple visuals. Use a whiteboard or a chart to track how many forms were processed per day, how long approvals sat in a queue, or how many errors had to be corrected. Let the team see the numbers change. That creates ownership. It also gives you something real to share with leaders.

4. Be consistent with how you measure. Do not change the definition halfway through. If you are tracking time from intake to completion, stick with that. If you are measuring number of handoffs, do not start including phone calls unless that was part of the original count. Consistency builds trust in the numbers.

5. Use language that leadership understands. If the change saved 40 hours a month, say it. If it reduced rework by 30 percent, say that too. But also say what that time was used for. Were more clients served? Did it reduce backlog? Did it free up people to focus on work that was previously delayed? Translate the outcome into what it allowed the business to do better.

6. Finally, document it. Use a one page summary that includes what was improved, how it was measured, what changed, and what the team learned. You are not writing a report. You are building a habit of showing results clearly. This becomes your proof, ot for justifying what was done but also for making the case to do more.

Step 2: Translate impact into financial terms

Once you know what changed, the next step is to make it mean something to the people who control the budget. That means turning operational results into financial language. Time, effort, and rework are not free. They cost money. If you want Lean to move beyond the team level, you have to show what those improvements are worth in real terms. Not in theory. In dollars.

Start by identifying what the improvement affects. If you reduced cycle time, how many hours were saved? If error rates dropped, how much rework was avoided? If work volume went up without adding staff, what would it have cost to achieve that increase without the improvement? Use that logic. Keep it simple. You are not building a business case for an acquisition. You are showing how much waste used to cost and how much of that cost was removed.

> **Do not call everything savings**. Leaders know the difference between actual budget reduction and time freed up. Call it what it is. Hard savings reduce spend. Soft savings create capacity. Risk reduction protects against future cost. Clarify which one you are reporting. When you try to turn everything into hard dollars, people stop listening. But when you show how a process change avoided a new hire or eliminated overtime, that gets attention. That is what makes Lean real to decision makers.

Lean is not free. Training, time, and support all come at a cost. If you want more of it, you need to show what the organization got back. Use common cost categories. Labor hours. Contract spend. Scrap. Recovery time. You do not need finance to validate every line, but you do need enough structure to make your case hold up. If you are not sure how to value something, talk to the person who owns that area of the business. They will tell you what it costs to fix a defect, to hire a contractor, or to clean up a customer issue. Use their numbers. When you use the business's own math, you are more likely to be heard. You do not need to overcomplicate it. You need to make the connection between the change and the financial impact clear. If something got better, show what that improvement is worth. This is where Lean goes from being a team exercise to a leadership conversation. This is where momentum starts to scale.

Step 3: Share the full story

Once you have the data and the financial impact, you are not done. You still need to make it stick. That means telling the full story clearly and in a way that leadership can understand without needing a slide deck. If they cannot explain it to someone else in one sentence, it is not ready.

Start by saying what changed and why it matters. Then explain how it happened. What problem did the team see? What did they do about it? What was the result? That is the story. Not the tool. Not the Lean terms. Just the problem, the action, and the outcome. Keep it that simple. That kind of story spreads. People remember it. They start asking for more of it. It creates pull instead of relying on push.

Do not bury the lead. If rework dropped 40 percent and customer complaints were cut in half, say that first. Then explain what part of the process changed and how the team made it happen. Name the people involved. Let them tell it if you are presenting. When leaders hear results and see who made it happen, they stop seeing Lean as something to sponsor. They start seeing it as something that works. Include what else got better even if it is not tied to dollars. Did the team get time back? Did training get easier? Did stress levels go down? These outcomes show that Lean improves more than just the numbers. When you share both the results and the experience, you build trust. You are not selling a method. You are showing what happens when people use it to fix their own problems.

Keep it short. Keep it honest. Keep it real. You are not trying to impress. You are trying to prove Lean belongs in your organization. And the best way to do that is with a story the business can repeat without you in the room.

Step 4: Reinvest the gains

When a Lean effort delivers value, do not stop. Use what was gained to create the next improvement. This is how Lean becomes a system, not an event. You are not asking for more resources. You are showing how the results of one effort fund the next. That is what keeps Lean alive when the spotlight moves on.

Start by asking what the improvement made possible. If time was saved, where is that time being used now? If errors were reduced, what can the team focus on that used to get pushed aside? If customer issues dropped, how can that team now support a new area? These are the questions that show leadership this is not just savings. It is progress. You also make it clear that Lean is not about cutting. It is about making space for better work. When teams see that their effort gave them capacity, flexibility, or clarity, they are more likely to try again. When leaders see that results create new capability without new spend, they pay attention. You do not wait for approval to keep going. You bring the next problem forward. You show how it connects to the last one. You build from the same tools, use the same data, and follow the same approach. That consistency proves Lean is not a one time fix. It is how the work improves over time.

> Reinvestment is what makes improvement sustainable. You are not chasing savings. You are building a system where value funds value. That is how you move from isolated efforts to a culture that expects better and knows how to get there.

Back in my day. An author reflection.

Back in my day, when I was consulting for a global car rental company, I saw what it looks like when a leader actually knows how to drive cost efficiency the right way through Lean. This was not a small branch. It was one of their busiest locations, right outside a major airport. High volume. Constant movement. Every delay had a cost. Cars were coming in, but it was taking too long to turn them around. Cleaning, fueling, inspection, all of it. The hold ups meant more labor, more frustration, and too often, they had to bring in extra vehicles from nearby locations just to stay on track.

The regional manager did not open with a speech or a plan. He showed up and watched. Three days in the return lane with a clipboard and no attitude. He followed the cars. He talked to the porters, the cleaning crew, and the front office staff. He did not ask why they were behind. He asked what was slowing them down. That one question shifted the entire tone. No blame. Just curiosity. He worked with the team to lay out the steps. Not a training tool. Just a simple map of what happens from the time a car is dropped off to the time it is ready to go back out. They sketched it on a whiteboard in the breakroom. Then they walked the process. More than once. They noticed the real problem was not the work, it was the layout. Cleaning supplies were stored too far from the work area. The fuel key was locked inside the office. Cars waited in line at the wash bay because they were cleaned in batches instead of flow.

The manager did not cut hours or build a business case. He moved the cleaning station closer. He gave the fuel key to the person already walking that path. He worked with the team to adjust the cleaning checklist so it matched the actual steps the team followed. These were small changes that removed friction. That was the point. It took twelve minutes off each turnaround. With the volume they were running, that meant hundreds of hours back each week. Cars were ready sooner. Fewer were pulled in from outside. The cost dropped without touching the budget. He tracked the improvement on a whiteboard. Three numbers. Time from drop off to ready, how many cars were available by each shift, and how many had to be brought in from other sites. The moment the numbers improved, he handed the marker to the team. From that day on, they owned the results.

That is what cost efficiency through Lean actually looks like. Not a new system. Not a workshop. Just a leader willing to see the work, ask the right questions, and clear the path. It was not fancy. But it worked. And it stayed.

In Summary

Cost gets attention. It always has. But that is not why Lean works. Lean works because it connects action to impact and makes improvement real. When leaders can see the results, when teams can feel the difference, and when the business runs better because of it, that is what earns the right to keep going. Cost is the proof. But purpose is the reason. And metrics are what bridge the two.

That bridge matters. Because not everything that counts can be counted. And not everything that can be counted counts. The job is not to measure everything. It is to measure what matters and make sure everyone knows why it matters. That is how you build alignment. That is how you avoid chasing numbers that mean nothing. And that is how you lead with purpose instead of pressure.

So before we talk about culture, we need to talk about metrics. Not just how to track them, but how to choose them, how to use them, and how to keep them from becoming the goal instead of the guide. Let's walk into that next.

Chapter Three

The Role of Metrics and Purpose

Some teams measure everything. Some measure nothing. Neither is leading. Both are guessing. This chapter is not about tracking more data. It is about choosing what matters and turning it into something the team can see, understand, and act on. That is the job. Not collecting. Connecting.

Good metrics are not about proving performance. They are about improving it. That means you do not start with the system. You start with the purpose. What are we trying to build? What behavior do we want to support? Until you can answer that, no metric will help. Once you can, the right measure becomes obvious.

> The tools are not the point. The graph is not the point. The goal is to build a system that shows the team what success looks like and helps them see when the process is slipping. It should not require a dashboard to interpret. It should be obvious. Visual. Useful. It should pull people into the work and hold up a mirror to how it is really running.

In this chapter, we are going to walk through three parts: choosing what to measure, choosing how to measure, and creating visual management. Not theory. Not reports. Just grounded leadership. Done well, it turns the invisible into action. Done poorly, it just adds noise.

Choosing What to Measure

Most metrics are chosen for the wrong reason. Someone above asked for them. A report needed a number. A vendor had a dashboard. That is not leadership. That is compliance. Good leaders do not measure what is easy. They measure what matters.

You start by asking one question: What is the purpose of this process? Not the output. The purpose. What value is it supposed to deliver? Who is it for? What would good look like to them? If you cannot answer those questions, you are not ready to measure. Metrics are not about the team. They are about the customer. Internal or external.

If the goal is speed, measure time. If the goal is accuracy, measure errors. If the goal is trust, measure consistency. But pick one. Do not chase everything. One of the fastest ways to build clarity is to measure less. Pick the core behavior that drives success and lock in on that.

For example, a support team is measured on handle time. So they rush calls. But the real goal is customer resolution. If that is the case, measure first call resolution instead. Watch what happens. Behavior follows measurement. Get the measure right, and the system starts working the way it should. Also ask what *not* to measure. Some numbers feel safe but do more harm than good. They drive fear. They drive hiding. They turn the work into a game of optics. You do not need ten dashboards. You need a few honest *signals*. If the metric creates noise, it is not helping.

Ask:

1. Does this measure reflect what matters most?

2. Does it drive the right behavior?

3. Will the team trust it?

If the answer is no, stop there. You are not ready to move forward.

Choosing How to Measure

Once you know what to measure, the next step is figuring out how. This is where most systems get too complex or too casual. One turns into bureaucracy. The other turns into noise. Good leaders find the middle. They pick an approach that is accurate enough to see the truth and simple enough to keep using.

The first rule is measure close to the work. The farther the data is from the process, the more distorted it gets. If you are tracking cycle time, do not rely on the date it hits the system and the date it exits. That leaves out the gaps. The handoffs. The holds. You want the time the work starts and the time it finishes. Measure what the team feels.

The second rule is measure consistently. A metric that changes definitions every week is worse than no metric at all. You cannot coach a moving target. Define what counts. Define when to count it. Define how to collect it. Then protect that clarity. Especially when the pressure is on. Metrics without standards become weapons.

For example, a leader tracks errors by category but lets each team define categories their own way. So one team counts missing fields as data errors. Another counts them as training. Another does not count them at all. The number is not helping. It is hiding the truth. A shared measure requires shared language. Also, be mindful of how data gets collected. If it depends on memory, it is probably wrong. If it is pulled from a system no one trusts, it will be ignored. If it is collected by someone far from the work, it will miss the nuance. The best data is built into the process itself. It does not require extra steps. It just gets captured.

Ask:

1. Is this how the team would measure it?

2. Does this method reveal the truth or protect the optics?

3. Can we teach this method in five minutes or less?

If not, simplify it. You are not building a data warehouse. You are leading with facts. Make the facts easy to see and hard to ignore.

THE ROLE OF METRICS AND PURPOSE

Creating Visual Management

Once you know what to measure and how to measure it, you need to make it visible. Not in a dashboard that only a few people check. Not in a spreadsheet buried in a folder. Visible means public. Immediate. Part of the daily rhythm. That is what makes it useful.

Visual management is not about color coding. It is not about style. It is about focus. It helps people see the truth and act on it without delay. Done right, it becomes part of how the team thinks. A wall of data that tells you what matters. A signal system that says if the work is on track or off.

Start with this: can someone walk by and tell if we are winning? That is the test. If you need a meeting or a report to answer that, your system is not visual. The goal is not to update leadership. The goal is to let the team lead themselves.

For example, a service team tracks request completion. Every day, they update a whiteboard with the number finished, the number started, and the number stuck. Green for done. Yellow for in progress. Red for blocked. No login. No refresh. Just walk up and see. It is not fancy. It works.

As another example, a team builds a Pareto chart of the top issues causing delays. They update it weekly with a marker and tape. The biggest bar is where they focus that week. Everyone sees it. Everyone knows the plan. It is not digital. It is visible.

Ask these questions:

1. Can the team see the metric without asking?

2. Can they tell if it is normal or off track?

3. Do they know what action to take if it is off?

If the answer is no, the visual system is not working. Clarity is not decoration. It is discipline. The easier it is to see, the harder it is to ignore. That is what makes visual management powerful. It keeps the truth in the open. It gives the team control. And it keeps leaders honest.

> Visuals should not become wallpaper. If they stop helping, change them. If they stop being used, ask why. If they confuse more than clarify, simplify. Visual management is not a one-time setup. It is a living part of the work. Keep it close to the action. Keep it easy to update. Keep it real.

Let's make this easier to use. Simple. Practical. Repeatable. The LENS model gives you a way to focus your thinking when it comes to measurement. It is not a checklist. It is a lens, something you look through to sharpen your view. Each part helps you test whether your metrics are doing their job. Leading the right behavior. Exposing the real story. Nudging the system forward.

The LENS Model: A Leader's Guide to Operational Clarity

Locate the Work. **E**xpress the Standard. **N**ame the Measure. **S**how the Truth. Each step builds on the last. Each one forces a moment of clarity. Not about the tools. About the work. About what matters. This model is not a checklist. It is a habit. A way to see the system clearly and lead from what is real.

L – Locate the Work

Before you measure anything, know where the value lives. Go to the work. Not the meeting room. Not the inbox. Where the service is delivered. Where the product is built. Where the experience is felt. That is where measurement starts.

Ask:

1. What part of the work creates value?

2. Where do customers feel the impact most?

3. Where do delays, waste, or rework hide?

This step ensures you are not measuring what is easy. You are measuring what matters.

E – Express the Standard

Once you find the work, define what good looks like. Not in vague terms. In clear, observable behavior. This is the gap most leaders skip. They measure output without defining the process. That invites chaos. This step grounds the system.

Ask:

1. What does success look like here?

2. What is the expected way the work should run?

3. What would "normal" feel like for the team doing it?

This gives you a baseline. A place to measure from. Without a standard, every number is noise.

N – Name the Measure

Now that you have the standard, pick the measure. Just one or two. Not ten. Focus beats coverage. Choose what shows the health of the system, not just the result. Think behavior over outcome. Rhythm over spike.

Ask:

1. What one measure would tell me if the system is working?

2. What would the team look at daily and say, "this tells our story"?

3. What is leading indicator, not just lagging result?

Choose measures that create action, not just reflection. Make them visible. Make them simple. Make them matter.

S – Show the Truth

This is where visual management comes in. Build a signal system. Not a report. A visual. Something people see without clicking. Something that updates without delay. Make the truth easy to find and hard to ignore.

Ask:

1. Can the team see the current state at a glance?

2. Can they tell if we are winning, drifting, or stuck?

3. Can they take action without waiting for permission?

Put the measure where the work lives. Keep it physical if possible. Let it pull people into the problem before it becomes a crisis. Use it to lead. Not to report. Not to punish. To lead.

The LENS Model in Action

Imagine a call center struggling with slow response times. A leader using the LENS model might:

1. *Locate the Work:* Spend time with reps, listen to live calls, see the queue build.

2. *Express the Standard:* Define that a good day means 90% of calls answered in under 60 seconds.

3. *Name the Measure:* Choose "calls answered under 60 seconds per hour" as the metric.

4. *Show the Truth:* Build a daily board that shows performance by hour in red or green. No logins. No hiding.

> Now the team owns the number. They see when it slips. They act when it drifts. The leader does not push. The system pulls.

Why This Works

The LENS model keeps the leader focused on what matters. It protects against vanity metrics. It turns performance into behavior. It makes the invisible visible. And it builds a culture of clarity without adding complexity. Most leaders want to improve. They just do not know where to look or how to see. This model helps them look through the noise and see the system. One step at a time. One question at a time. One truth at a time.

LENS Model Diagnostic: A tool for leaders to focus measurement, define standards, and lead with clarity.

1. Locate the Work

Go where the value is created. Answer these questions:

1. What is the core value this team delivers?

2. Where does that value actually get created or delayed?

3. Who sees the impact when things go wrong?

If you cannot point to the real work, you are not ready to measure it.

2. Express the Standard

Define what "good" looks like. Be clear and specific:

1. What behavior or output is expected when the process is running well?

2. Can every person doing the work describe what success looks like?

3. Do we all agree on what normal feels like?

If there is no standard, there is no stability. Do not measure yet.

3. Name the Measure

Choose one or two metrics. Not five. Not ten. Focus on what drives performance:

    1. What metric tells you if the process is working the way it should?

    2. Is it timely? Is it visible? Is it tied to behavior, not just results?

    3. Will this measure help the team act or just reflect after the fact?

If it does not help people act in real time, it is not a useful measure.

4. Show the Truth

Check the visual management system. Truth should be obvious and immediate:

    1. Can the team see the current state without asking for a report?

    2. Can they tell if we are on track, slipping, or off course at a glance?

    3. Does the visual pull people into the right conversation without a meeting?

If it's hidden behind a login or delayed by a report, it is not helping you lead.

Reflection

Based on your answers above, where is your biggest gap?

- I have not located the work clearly.

- I need to define the standard.

- I am measuring too much or the wrong thing.

- The truth is not visible or actionable.

What is one step I will take this week to close that gap?

> This diagnostic is not about judgment. It is about focus. Use it in one-on-ones. Use it in team huddles. Use it when the system feels loud and the truth feels far away.

In Summary

The LENS model is not another framework to memorize. It is a way to think. A way to keep your eyes on the work, not just the numbers. It helps you choose measures that matter, track them in ways that drive clarity, and build habits that keep truth visible. That is what measurement is for. Not performance reviews. Not dashboards. Better decisions. Better action. Better learning.

But measurement only gets you so far. Because sooner or later, you run into the real constraints: power, influence, and approval. The people above you. That is where a lot of good work stalls. Not because the idea is wrong. Because the support is missing. The next chapter is about how to manage up without watering things down. Without becoming a translator or a shield. You do not have to compromise to lead. But you do need to know how to navigate. Let's walk through how.

Chapter Four

Managing Up Without Compromise

A lot of Lean work never sees the light of day. Not because the team gave up. Because the layers above them said no. Or maybe they said nothing. Just silence, delay, or "not right now." That is the moment where most systems stall. Not at the idea. At the approval. This chapter is about how to lead when you are not the final word. When your hands are tied but your head is still clear.

Managing up is not about selling. It is not about making the case so perfect that no one can say no. It is about staying honest while being strategic. It is about sharing the truth of the work without backing down or dressing it up. This is not politics. This is alignment. Done right, managing up is not about avoiding tension. It is about knowing *how to use it*. Let's get into it.

Know What You're Asking For

Before you step into the room, slow down and get clear. Not on your frustration. Not on your opinion. On your ask. What are you actually bringing forward? What do you need them to do? Make a decision? Approve a change? Remove a blocker? Most upward conversations stall because that part is fuzzy. The leader listens, nods, thanks you for the update.....and nothing changes. Not because they did not care. Because you never told them **what action was needed**.

This is not about being forceful. It is about being focused. You are not there to dump issues or vent stress. You are there to lead. That means walking in with intent. The clearer your ask, the sharper the conversation. It moves faster. It stays grounded. And it builds trust, because you're not wasting their time or yours.

If you are not sure what the ask is, you are not ready to go up the chain. Sit with it. Write it out. Test it with someone you trust. Make sure your team knows too. The best way to build credibility at the next level is to model clarity at yours.

Speak in System Terms

When you talk up the chain, talk in systems. Not anecdotes. Not emotions. Not "we're drowning down here." Executives deal in systems and levers. If you want traction, speak in the language they live in. That means showing how the issue connects to throughput, risk, cost, or experience. That means naming the process that is breaking down, not just the symptom you're feeling.

This is not about sounding smart. It is about being useful. The leader you're speaking to has to decide where to put their attention. If your message is vague or personal, it feels like noise. But if you name the pattern, if you frame the system, if you tie the problem to the health of the operation, they listen. They can act.

Practice this before you go in. Say it out loud. "The intake process is causing rework across three teams." That is different from "we're always redoing things." One gets a reaction. The other gets remembered.

You are not just managing up. You are inviting partnership. Speak in systems and you show them where to help.

Clarify the Ask

Never walk into a leadership conversation just to vent. Go in with a clear ask. What do you need them to do? Approve a change? Remove a blocker? Set a priority? Be specific. Executives make decisions all day. If your message is unclear, it gets set aside.

That does not mean you have to come in with a full solution. But it does mean you need to be crisp about what matters right now. "We need approval to run a short pilot" is better than "we're thinking about trying something." "We need clarity on which metric takes precedence" is stronger than "the goals are confusing." The difference is intent.

A clear ask shows you are not just surfacing problems. You are owning them. It signals that you are not waiting to be rescued. You are leading and inviting support.

The clearer you are, the easier it is to get a real answer. That saves time, builds trust, and moves the work forward.

Explain the Stakes Without Drama

Senior leaders do not respond to theatrics. They respond to clarity. When you explain the stakes, keep it sharp and grounded. Not "this is a disaster," but "if this continues, we risk a 20 percent drop in throughput within three weeks." Not "the team is falling apart," but "morale is dipping, and we are seeing more rework as a result."

The goal is not to scare them. The goal is to help them see what is at risk if nothing changes. Leaders make tradeoffs every day. They cannot do that well if you only bring emotion. They need context, urgency, and a sense of impact.

When you make the stakes clear without turning up the heat, you build credibility. You are not just managing up. You are framing the problem like a peer. That changes the dynamic. It makes the conversation about the system, not about stress. And it makes you someone they want to keep listening to.

Propose a Path, Not a Complaint

Leaders do not need more problems. They need people who can see the issue and offer a path forward. That does not mean having every answer. It means showing that you have thought about the next step. Bring one or two practical options. Outline the tradeoffs. Explain what is in your control and what is not. Then ask for support where it is needed.

This changes the conversation. You are not adding to their workload. You are making it easier for them to make a decision. It positions you as a partner, not a problem. The best way to manage up is to make it easy to say yes. That starts with showing you can lead through the issue, not just report it.

Hold the Standard in Both Directions

You do not lead up by backing down. You lead up by holding the standard with respect. That means being clear about what matters and why. If a leader is pushing for something that will harm the system, it is your job to say so. Not with attitude. With facts. With clarity. With calm.

This is not about defiance. It is about discipline. If your job is to protect the process, that means protecting it from pressure too. When you stay grounded in the work, when you show how cutting a corner today will cost more tomorrow, you are doing your job. You are not resisting leadership. You are being one.

Know When to Escalate and When to Absorb

Not every issue needs to be surfaced. Some friction is part of leadership. You will be given decisions you would not have made. You will see strategies you do not fully agree with. That does not mean they are wrong. It means your job is to lead through them.

But there is a line. When a direction threatens the integrity of the system or the well-being of your people, it is time to escalate. When that happens, do it with clarity and respect. Frame it as a shared goal. Use facts. Keep the tone steady. And be ready to stand by your reasoning.

Leadership is not about shielding senior leaders from reality. But it is not about pushing every tension up the chain either. The skill is in knowing the difference. And the strength is in acting with purpose either way.

Protect the Team Without Becoming the Shield

It is noble to want to protect your team. But do not confuse protection with avoidance. If leaders above you are putting pressure on the system, your job is not to absorb it and let your team work in the dark. Your job is to translate that pressure into clarity. To share what is happening in a way that empowers, not paralyzes.

Do not take all the heat. Teach your team how to handle it. Let them see the realities without letting it crush them. This is how you build resilience. Not by sheltering people, but by giving them the tools and truth to face the work head on. Managing up without compromise means managing through without distortion.

Managing Up Diagnostic: Pressure vs. Principle

> This is not a quiz. It is a mirror. Read each question and answer honestly based on your current behavior. The goal is not perfection. The goal is clarity.

1. When leadership pressures the team to move faster or cut steps, how do you respond?

☐ I push it down and hope the team absorbs it.

☐ I translate the ask into action while protecting the standard.

☐ I freeze or avoid taking a position.

2. When you see a direction that could harm the system, what do you do?

☐ I stay quiet, pushing back feels risky.

☐ I raise it respectfully, with data and alternatives.

☐ I escalate only when absolutely unavoidable.

3. How often do you bring solutions, not just problems, to senior leaders?

☐ Rarely, I mostly report what's not working.

☐ Sometimes, I bring ideas but not fully formed.

☐ Consistently, I come with tradeoffs and paths forward.

4. What is your instinct when a decision from above conflicts with your values or process standards?

☐ I vent privately and try to work around it.

☐ I surface the issue professionally and stand by the process.

☐ I go along but it stays with me.

5. When you shield your team, is it in a way that makes them stronger or softer?

☐ I buffer everything, they should focus on the work.

☐ I share pressure with context so they build resilience.

☐ I withhold tough truths to keep morale high.

6. Do you speak about leadership decisions with the same clarity and calm whether you agree or not?

☐ No, it's hard to mask my frustration.

☐ Usually, I try, but sometimes it leaks.

☐ Yes, I stay grounded and focused on the mission.

7. Do you know when to escalate an issue and when to absorb it?

☐ Not really, I either escalate everything or nothing.

☐ I guess, but I second-guess often.

☐ Yes, I know what belongs where and why.

> Which question felt most uncomfortable? That is your signal. Not to feel bad. To get better. Managing up is not about pleasing people or resisting them. It is about leading from a grounded place, with calm, clarity, and conviction. If something in these questions gave you pause, that is not failure. That is awareness. Take it seriously. Take action. And lead with both courage and respect.

In Summary

The real test of leadership is not what you do when everyone agrees. It is what you do when the pressure climbs, the direction feels off, and the easy move is to stay quiet. Managing up without compromise means holding your ground without losing your posture. It means translating pressure into clarity and staying loyal to the process even when the ask from above feels misaligned. That does not mean defiance. It means discipline. The kind that earns trust up and down. The kind that makes you the person they want in the room when things get hard.

You are not here to play it safe. You are here to make it better. That takes courage. It takes calm. It takes a leader who can speak plainly and act wisely, especially when the stakes are high. That is the work. And it does not stop with one conversation or one stand. It shows up every day in how you show up, what you protect, and what you model.

Now that you have your footing, it is time to move from protection to creation. The next chapter shifts from managing up to building out. From defending the system to shaping it. Because once you can hold your ground, the next job is to grow it. Let's talk about how to build a real culture of problem solving, one where the tools work, the people think, and the system gets stronger because of you. Let's go.

Chapter Five

Building a Culture of Problem Solving

Most organizations do not have a problem solving culture. They have a problem escalation culture. When something goes wrong, people look up the chain for answers. They wait. They ask for direction. They pass it on. Not because they are unwilling to solve it, but because the culture has taught them to play it safe. Solving problems feels like a risk. Escalating them feels like the rule.

That is not how Lean works. Lean pushes problem solving as close to the work as possible. The people doing the work see the problems first. They experience the frustration. They know what is broken. A strong Lean culture does not tell them to escalate it. It gives them the structure and support to fix it.

This chapter is about what it takes to build that kind of environment. Where problems are surfaced early, owned locally, and solved quickly. Not by a few experts, but by everyone. It is not about launching a new training program. It is about changing how people think, how they respond, and what they expect when something goes wrong. Culture is not built by chance. It is built by what you allow, what you reward, and what you repeat. Let's walk through how to build a culture where solving problems is not the exception. It is the expectation.

If you want problem solving to become part of the culture, you cannot leave it to chance. You have to build it with intention. That means setting clear expectations, removing barriers, and showing people what good looks like. It does not happen through a workshop. It happens through repeated behaviors. The model below is not a checklist. It is a practical way to shift how people think about problems and how they respond when they see one. If you follow these steps consistently, the culture starts to shift. Not because you told people to solve problems, but because you showed them how and backed them when they did.

The Five Step Model to Create a Problem Solving Culture

Step 1: Make problems visible

You cannot fix what people are afraid to show. If problems stay hidden, they stay unsolved. Most organizations are not short on issues, they are short on visibility. The problems are there, but no one wants to say it out loud. People get used to workarounds or containments. They stop bringing things up because nothing changes or because they do not want to be seen as negative. That silence becomes the culture.

The first step to building a problem solving environment is breaking that silence. You have to create space where problems are expected, not avoided. That starts with how you ask. Do not ask if everything is going well. Ask what is getting in the way. Ask what is not working as intended. Ask where the work is harder than it should be. These are the questions that get real answers. Use a visible method to track what comes up. A simple board. A running list. A shared space where the team can raise what they are seeing.

The format does not matter. What matters is that everyone knows it is safe to speak up and that raising a problem is the first step, not a risk. You also have to respond the right way when someone brings something forward. Do not debate it. Do not downplay it. Just listen. Ask questions to understand. If the problem is real, make sure it stays on the radar. If it is a misunderstanding, clarify it respectfully. How you react sets the tone for what comes next.

Over time, when people see that problems are heard, discussed, and acted on, they start bringing them forward without being asked. That is the shift. That is when visibility becomes habit. And once the problems are visible, you can start fixing them. But it does not happen unless someone feels safe enough to name the first one.

Step 2: Push ownership to the source

Once problems are visible, the next step is deciding who owns them. In most organizations, that responsibility moves up the chain. The more visible the issue, the more senior the person who gets assigned to it. That may sound efficient, but it slows everything down and disconnects the people who actually understand the problem from the chance to solve it.

Lean works differently. It puts the responsibility for fixing problems as close to the work as possible. If the issue happens on the front line, the team on the front line should be the first to take a shot at solving it. They live with the process. They feel the friction. They see what triggers the delays and where the confusion starts. That insight is the edge. This is not about making people do more. It is about making it normal to improve what you own. You are not asking for a presentation. You are asking for action. When a team sees something is broken and knows they are expected to fix it, it changes how they see their role. They stop waiting and start working.

To make this work, leaders have to stop jumping in too fast. Do not take the problem from the team. Ask what they have already tried. Ask what they think is causing it. Ask what would make it better. Guide the thinking, but do not take over. When leaders hold back just enough, it gives the team room to step up. Ownership does not come from assigning blame. It comes from trust. And when teams are trusted to own the fix, they start building the confidence to solve bigger problems over time. That is how a culture of problem solving begins to take root. Not through more oversight. Through more ownership.

Step 3: Provide simple structure

Once a team owns the problem, they need a way to work through it. Not a full training course. Not a binder of tools. Just a simple structure that helps them think clearly and take action. This is where a lot of organizations overcomplicate the work. They introduce advanced terms, require long templates, or gate improvement behind approval. That kills momentum. It turns solving problems into more process.

Lean is not about complexity. It is about clarity. The structure should be simple enough that anyone can use it, and strong enough that it leads to real action. Start with the basics. What is the problem? Why does it matter? What do we think is causing it? What can we try to improve it? What happened when we did? You do not need more than that. Use the five whys. Sketch a basic before and after. Write it on a whiteboard. Talk it out in ten minutes. The point is not to run a project. It is to move the work forward. The structure is there to guide the thinking, not to slow it down.

This also builds consistency. When every team uses the same approach to think through a problem, it becomes easier to coach, easier to track, and easier to repeat. You do not need a problem solving team. You need a team that knows how to solve problems. Simple structure removes excuses. It gives people a place to start. And when the process is easy to follow, people are more likely to use it again. That is what builds habit. That is how problem solving becomes part of the way the work gets done. Not by accident. By design.

Step 4: Respond the right way

How a leader responds when someone brings up a problem decides everything that happens next. It sets the tone. It tells people whether speaking up is worth the risk. If the first reaction is blame, dismissal, or indifference, that shuts it down. People go quiet. They stop trying. But if the response is interest, support, and respect, people start to believe it is safe to speak up and expected to act.

You do not need to fix the problem. You need to show up the right way when it is raised. Ask questions. What are you seeing? What have you tried? What do you think would help? What do you need from me? These questions put the focus back on the team and keep ownership where it belongs. You are not taking the work. You are making it possible. When the team acts, respond to the effort. If it worked, make it visible. If it did not, ask what was learned. Either way, you show the team that solving problems is part of the job. You reinforce that progress matters more than perfection.

> You do not build culture with posters or policies. You build it with your reactions. Every time someone raises an issue or takes a step to fix it, how you respond either builds trust or breaks it. The right response turns a one-time effort into a habit. That is how problem solving becomes normal. That is how it sticks.

Step 5: Celebrate the fix, not the failure

Most organizations shine a spotlight on problems when something breaks. Metrics drop. Customers complain. Leaders respond. The focus is on what went wrong and who owns it. That does not build a problem solving culture. It builds a culture of fear and reaction. If you want people to keep solving problems, you need to make a bigger deal out of the fix than the failure.

When a team improves something, talk about it. Show what changed. Let them explain how they did it. Not in a formal presentation. Just a short summary of the problem, the action, and the result. Give them the credit. Make it part of your staff meetings, team huddles, or one on ones. These stories become the examples that others follow. Keep it simple. The fix does not have to be huge. Maybe they reduced handoffs. Maybe they fixed a delay. Maybe they made a form clearer so fewer people had to call for help. The size does not matter. What matters is that they saw something was broken and took ownership to make it better.

When you highlight these efforts, you are sending a clear message. This is what we do here. We do not wait. We do not escalate everything. We fix what we can. When that becomes what people see, it becomes what they do. Culture does not shift because of one big win. It shifts when people see small improvements being noticed, valued, and repeated. Celebrate the fix. Make it public. Make it normal. That is how you build a culture where solving problems is not extra work. It is just work.

Leader Reflection: Do You Create a Culture of Problem Solving?

Take ten minutes. No slides. No filters. Just answer the questions below for yourself. This is not about grading your leadership. It is about holding up a mirror. Your actions, not your intent, shape the culture around you.

1. When a problem comes up, how do you respond?

Do you ask questions or start solving? Do you clear the way or take the work? Think about your last three responses. Were they helpful, or did they stall momentum?

2. Do people feel safe speaking up?

When was the last time someone brought up a problem without being asked? How did you respond? How did others react after that? If no one is raising issues, do not assume everything is fine. Ask yourself what might be keeping them quiet.

3. Who actually owns the problems on your team?

Do issues stay with the people closest to the work, or do they always move up? Think about the last few things that broke. Who fixed them? If it was always you, why is that? What needs to change so the team takes the lead?

4. What structure do your teams actually use to solve problems?

Not what is on the shelf. What they actually use. Can your team walk through a basic method without a template or meeting? If not, what is in the way? Where can you simplify?

5. Do you recognize the fix, or just track what failed?

In your last team meeting, what got the most attention? Did you highlight what was improved, or just what broke? Do people know that solving problems gets noticed, or do they only hear about gaps?

> **Your Next Step:** Pick one answer that needs to change. Write down the habit or behavior that is getting in the way. Then decide what you will do differently this week. No plan. No pilot. Just one pattern you will shift through action. That is how culture changes. One behavior at a time. Repeated. Backed by you. Not announced. Just done.

In Summary

Building a culture of problem solving is not about permission. It is about expectation. You are not hoping people will step up. You are creating the conditions where stepping up is just how things work. That culture takes shape through visibility, local ownership, simple structures, and the right response. It grows through repetition, what gets reinforced, what gets supported, what gets done. But culture gets tested when things break. When the pressure spikes. When uncertainty takes over. That is when Lean either holds or folds. The next chapter is about those moments. When crisis hits. When fear shows up. When the plan does not fit the moment. It is not enough to build culture. You have to lead it through the fire. Let's talk about what that takes.

Chapter Six

Leading Lean in Crisis

Anyone can lead when things are calm. It is during crisis that leadership shows. Not the title. Not the tools. The behavior. The thinking. The choices that get made when time is short and stakes are high. That is when people look up. That is when culture either holds or collapses. And that is when Lean either disappears or proves its worth.

Crisis puts pressure on everything. Systems strain. Habits fray. Fear takes up space where clarity used to be. Leaders start reacting. Teams start guessing. The noise gets loud. And in that moment, Lean can feel like a luxury. Like something to pause until the fire is out. But that is the mistake. Because Lean is not for the easy days. It is for the hard ones. It is the structure that lets you focus. The discipline that cuts through chaos. The mindset that turns panic into action.

This chapter is not about surviving. It is about leading. When the plan breaks. When the numbers drop. When everything that worked yesterday no longer works today. That is not the time to abandon Lean. That is the time to lean into it. Not the slogans. The practice. The behaviors that anchor teams when everything else feels unstable.

We are going to walk through what that looks like. What changes. What holds. What strong leaders do differently when everything is on the line. Because Lean is not about control. It is about clarity. And when clarity is hardest to find, that is when it matters most. Let's get into it.

Returning to Purpose When Pressure Mounts

Crisis reveals what was already weak. It does not invent dysfunction. It exposes it. When pressure mounts, teams default to what they know. That is why purpose matters. Not as a phrase. Not as a slide. But as the anchor. When the ground shifts, it is the one thing that should not.

In normal times, purpose can feel like a luxury. A shared belief we revisit at offsites or town halls. But in crisis, it becomes a filter. It tells you what to keep. What to pause. What to ignore. The hard part is not acting. The hard part is choosing. Because in crisis, everything shows up screaming. Every leader feels the pull to do more. To help more. To fix everything. But that response creates noise, not clarity. It exhausts the team. It breaks the system.

When you lead with purpose, you do not remove the pressure. You redirect it. You remind people why their work matters when the outcomes get blurry. You reinforce what the organization stands for when trust starts to wobble. You keep decisions grounded in what is essential instead of what is loud.

If the team is stretched thin, purpose helps them choose which ball to drop. That is leadership. Not pretending everything can still happen. But helping people get clear on what cannot be missed.

Purpose is not just a statement. It is a standard. In a crisis, it is the one thing you do not compromise. You do not cut safety to save time. You do not skip the patient to protect the schedule. You do not chase cost at the expense of care. That is how trust dies. That is how systems collapse.

The question is simple. When it all hit the fan, what did we still protect? That answer tells you what kind of organization you really are.

Lean leaders use purpose as more than a message. They use it as a tool. To guide the decisions that matter. To calm the chaos. To steady the team. Not with speeches. With focus. That is the job when crisis comes. Not to control the storm. But to hold the line on what will not move.

Staying Disciplined When Urgency Takes Over

Crisis makes everything feel urgent. That is what makes it dangerous. Urgency pushes people to skip steps, cut corners, and call it being responsive. It does not feel like a choice. It feels like survival. But that urgency does not always help. Sometimes it just burns energy without fixing anything.

This is where discipline matters. Not rigid processes. Not bureaucracy. Real discipline. The kind that keeps people from making the same decision five different ways. The kind that keeps the work from falling apart just because the pace picked up.

> Lean systems do not collapse in crisis. They flex. They shorten feedback loops. They focus the daily work. They do not throw out the structure. They lean into it. Because that structure is what gives teams something to hold onto when the pressure builds. It keeps the thinking grounded when emotions run hot.

The myth is that standard work slows you down. That problem solving takes too long. That asking why is a waste of time when the fire is already burning. But that is how you end up solving the same fire twice. Or ten times. Or forever.

Leaders in crisis have to make fast decisions. But fast is not the same as frantic. You do not lose time by asking the right question before you act. You save it. Because if you solve the wrong thing, you just created more work.

The teams that hold up in crisis are not the ones who move the fastest. They are the ones who stay aligned. Who make decisions the same way. Who do not swing from idea to idea every time the pressure shifts. They have a center. And that center is discipline.

Discipline does not mean waiting. It means working with intention. It means having a plan for how decisions get made and how problems get solved, even when the plan changes. It means showing the team that chaos does not get to make the rules. We do.

Protecting Your People While Still Driving Performance

Crisis does not pause expectations. Deadlines still come. Customers still need answers. Leaders still feel the pull to deliver results. But here is the hard part, your team is not a machine. They are people. And crisis hits people first.

When stress goes up, focus goes down. When fear rises, trust gets thin. Leaders who forget this try to drive harder. Push for more. Demand resilience without recognizing the cost. That does not build strength. It builds burnout.

The goal is not to choose between people and performance. The goal is to protect both. That means showing your team that you see them. That you are not blind to the pressure. That you understand the strain. Then backing that up with action.

It means cutting the noise so the team can focus. It means tightening priorities so they are not pulled in ten directions. It means removing waste from meetings, updates, and reporting so time can go to the work that matters. It means making it okay to name what is hard without being seen as weak.

> Performance does not come from pressure. It comes from clarity. It comes from the team knowing exactly what matters and exactly how to respond. Your job is to build that clarity. To protect the system that protects the people so they can keep moving forward without burning out.

When leaders protect the team's focus, energy, and trust, performance follows. Not because the pressure is gone. But because the team believes they can handle it and they know you are with them when they do.

Making the Hard Call Without Losing the Team

Crisis forces decisions. Not just fast ones. Hard ones. The kind that affect people, priorities, and sometimes the future of the organization itself. These are not theoretical choices. They are real trade-offs. And leaders cannot avoid them.

But, there is a difference between making the hard call and making it alone. Between acting quickly and acting recklessly. Between moving forward and leaving your team behind.

The goal in crisis is not consensus. It is clarity. The team does not need to vote. They need to understand. Why this decision. Why now. Why it matters. If you do not explain that, they will fill in the blanks. And when fear writes the story, trust breaks fast.

This is not about oversharing. It is about transparency. Enough detail so people know the logic behind the choice. Enough honesty so they know where things stand. Enough conviction so they know you are not guessing your way through it.

And when the call affects people, when roles shift, work gets cut, or jobs are on the line, this is where leadership matters most. Not in the announcement. In the aftermath. In the way you listen. In the way you answer. In the way you treat the people impacted. That is what shapes culture. Not the decision, but how you show up after you make it.

Hard calls come with weight. Carry it in the open. Carry it with clarity. And carry it in a way that makes your team stronger even when the answer is hard.

Staying Anchored in Purpose When the Pressure Mounts

Crisis pulls leaders in every direction. Noise gets louder. Fire drills become the norm. The pressure to deliver rises fast and rarely lets up. In that chaos, it is easy to lose your anchor. To stop asking what matters and start chasing what moves.

But Lean leadership does not drift. It holds. Especially when everything else feels unstable. That steadiness does not come from confidence. It comes from clarity. Clarity of purpose. Clarity of values. Clarity of how you want to lead no matter what hits next.

> When pressure mounts, weak systems fold. So do weak principles. You will hear things like "just this once," "we'll go back later," "this is different." And maybe it is. But if you start trading your purpose for short-term wins, you do not get to keep calling it Lean. You just get chaos with good intentions.

That is why purpose must be visible. Written on the wall. Spoken in meetings. Used as a decision filter. It is the question behind the question, "Will this move us toward what we said we wanted to be?" If the answer is no, it is not the right move. Not even now.

And when the moment passes, because it always does, what will be left is the team that watched how you led through it. They will remember if you made the numbers or missed them. But they will follow you if they saw you lead with purpose anyway.

Hold the line. Not because it is easy. But because it is who you are as a leader.

Back in my day. An author reflection.

Back in my day, I was on a project back East, working with a global insurance company that had taken a federal bailout during the financial crisis. Their name was in the news. Their balance sheet was under scrutiny. And every move they made was being watched by the Fed.

It was not business as usual. The tone in the building was different. Fear was thick. Leadership meetings felt like courtrooms. Every decision needed a justification. Every fix had to show a return. It was not enough to be right. You had to be provably right. On paper. On schedule. And under pressure.

I was brought in as a principal consultant to help stabilize operations. But the real job was to help leaders think clearly again. Not just about metrics. About people. About flow. About priorities. Everyone was reacting. Understandably. But in the scramble to fix everything, they were breaking more than they were building.

So we slowed it down. Not the work. The thinking. We rebuilt visual management from scratch so teams could see where things stood without waiting for reports. We narrowed the focus to three critical outcomes. Not ten. Three. We taught leaders to stop chasing fires and start watching patterns. And we asked one question every day: What would still matter if the crisis ended tomorrow?

That question changed the tone. It turned noise into signal. It gave people permission to ignore distractions and focus on what would last. The Fed kept watching. The markets kept shifting. But inside the operation, something got steadier. The systems held. And so did the people.

That is the test of Lean in crisis. Not how much you change. How well you hold.

In Summary

Crisis does not change who we are. It reveals it. And for Lean leaders, that means resisting the urge to control through force and instead anchoring the system in clarity, simplicity, and trust. The best response to chaos is not more noise. It is calm repetition of what works. What matters. What lasts.

When the pressure is highest, strong systems protect people. Clear visuals keep the work visible. Steady routines create focus. And leaders show up not with answers, but with structure, giving the team a way to keep moving forward without guessing or burning out.

That is why Lean holds in crisis. Not because it has all the right tools, but because it builds the right habits. Habits that make it easier to think clearly. To act deliberately. To recover faster. And that's what we'll turn to next.

Because even in calm times, culture does not stick because of posters or programs. It sticks because of habits. Small ones. Repeated often. Baked into how people work, how they talk, how they lead. Let's talk about how to build those loops. The kind that create cultural gravity. The kind that hold when no one is watching.

Chapter Seven

Habit Loops and Cultural Stickiness

Culture does not shift because you asked it to. It shifts when people start doing the same thing the same way for the same reason. Over and over. That is what builds weight. That is what holds shape. Not a change initiative. A habit loop.

Lean lives or dies in the habits. Not the posters. Not the plans. The habits. And the most overlooked part of sustaining Lean is not the complexity of the work. It is the simplicity of what gets repeated. That is what makes it stick. Culture is not what people believe. It is what they do without thinking.

> If you want a culture of problem solving, then problem solving needs a rhythm. If you want data to drive decision making, then charts need to show up in the same place at the same time with the same questions. Not forced. Not overengineered. Just consistent. Clear. Repeatable.

This chapter is about the loops. The ones that build trust. The ones that make it easier to do the right thing than to fall back on old patterns. We are going to look at how habits form, why they break, and what leaders can do to make the new way easier than the old way. Not by pushing. By wiring it in.

Let's start with the smallest unit of change. The loop. The cue. The behavior. The reward. And how a leader turns that into culture. One moment at a time.

The Anatomy of a Habit Loop

Culture is not what people say in meetings. It is not the posters on the wall or the values in the handbook. Culture is what people do without being told. That is what sticks. That is what leads. And at the center of all of it is habit. Not the big kind. Not the strategic kind. The daily, repeatable kind. The one that feels automatic. That is where behavior lives. That is where culture hides.

A habit loop has three parts. A cue. A behavior. A reward. It starts with a trigger, something that tells the brain, "do the thing." That could be a time of day, a person walking in, a meeting kicking off. Then comes the behavior. What people do without thinking. Finally, there is the reward. Not always a cookie or a cheer. Sometimes it is just the relief of getting it done. The avoidance of conflict. The hit of being right. That cycle repeats. And before long, it becomes the norm.

This matters more than most leaders realize. Because it explains why new behaviors do not stick just because someone said they should. If the old cue is still there and the old reward is still waiting, the old behavior is coming back. That is not resistance. That is the loop doing what loops do.

If you want to change the culture, you have to change the loop. You have to know what triggers the behavior, what reinforces it, and what needs to shift so the new habit has a chance. You do not need a transformation plan. You need to look closer at what people do on autopilot. That is where the work begins.

Let's keep going. Next, we'll look at where those habit loops live, in the defaults of the organization. Not the stated ones. The real ones.

Defaults Drive Behavior

Most leaders think people resist change. That is not quite true. People resist confusion. They resist disruption that feels unsafe or performative. But more often, they are simply following the default. The path of least resistance. The way things work when no one is looking. That is not laziness. That is design.

In every organization, defaults shape behavior. If the default is to escalate rather than solve, that is what people will do. If the default is to wait for approval, that becomes the rhythm. If the default is to meet every issue with a meeting, meetings will multiply. These are not decisions. They are patterns. And they are powerful.

> Changing the culture means finding the defaults and replacing them with better ones. Not with rules. With systems. With cues and rewards that make the right behavior easier and the wrong one harder. That means giving teams a visible, simple way to take action. It means making improvement part of how the day works, not something to fit in after.

If the default is silence, make speaking up the easiest choice. If the default is delay, build habits that reward speed. If the default is fixing the symptom, make the root cause visible and harder to ignore. Defaults do not care about your values. They follow your design. If you want new behavior, build a new default.

Next, we'll get into how to use signals, those small, clear reinforcements, to anchor the loop and keep the behavior going.

Signals and Reinforcement

Culture does not grow from slogans. It grows from signals. Small, repeatable cues that show what matters and what does not. What gets attention. What gets ignored. What gets celebrated. What gets brushed off. Over time, those signals shape behavior more than any formal policy.

If a team shares a fix and no one responds, the signal is clear: this is not worth your time. If someone calls out waste and leadership shows up to learn, the signal is just as clear: this matters. These moments seem small. But they are culture in motion. Not what we say. What we reward. What we reinforce. That is what sticks.

Signals do not have to be big. A thank you in front of others. A question that nudges someone to think deeper. A pause to ask how the problem was solved, not just what result was hit. These are the moments that keep the loop going. Cue. Behavior. Reinforcement. Repeat.

> As a leader, your job is to manage the signals. To ensure the feedback loops reward the right behaviors. Not by controlling every action. But by being deliberate in how you respond. When someone shares bad news, do you thank them or push them away? When a fix fails, do you ask what was learned or assign blame? These choices become the cues others follow.

Consistency matters more than intensity. A small signal, repeated over time, will do more to shape the culture than a big gesture once a year. People watch what you do. They take cues from how you act under pressure. That is where values get tested. That is where the real culture forms.

Next, we will look at how to close the loop with one of the most overlooked elements in culture-building: the reward.

The Reward Loop

Habits do not last without reward. Not because people are selfish. Because that is how the brain works. When a new behavior gets a positive return, even something small, it creates a loop. Cue leads to behavior. Behavior leads to a reward. The brain connects the dots. Do this again.

> But in most Lean efforts, we forget this. We celebrate big wins, but miss the chance to reinforce the small steps. We reward outcomes, but not the process that got us there. We talk about continuous improvement, but we do not always show that improvement gets noticed.

The reward does not have to be money or promotion. In fact, it should not be. The strongest rewards are human. A sense of ownership. The respect of peers. Being trusted to solve harder problems. A leader who pauses and says, "That made a difference." These are the signals that make the habit loop stick.

If you want problem solving to become culture, you have to close the loop. Make the work visible. Make the learning matter. Recognize the effort, not just the outcome. This is not about trophies. It is about traction. When people see that good problem solving gets good attention, they do more of it.

That is how cultures grow. Not through slogans. Through loops. Through the quiet, steady rhythm of cue, behavior, reward. That rhythm builds belief. That belief builds habits. And those habits, over time, become the way things are done.

Let's wrap the chapter and set up what's next, the practical shift from early momentum to lasting traction. The part where Lean becomes more than a project and starts showing up in how people think, act, and lead. Let's talk about *Scaling Without Losing the Soul*.

Chapter Eight

Scaling Without Losing the Soul

Lean does not fail because the tools are wrong. It fails because the soul gets lost in the spread. What starts as focused, grounded, and meaningful turns into a rollout. Leaders get assigned instead of bought in. Teams get trained instead of invited. Metrics get pushed instead of owned. And somewhere in that expansion, the thing that made it work gets diluted.

This chapter is about protecting that soul. About scaling Lean in a way that keeps it human, keeps it honest, and keeps it tied to purpose. It is not about how many people you train. It is about how many people believe. It is not about how fast you spread. It is about how deep it roots.

We are going to walk through what it means to scale with integrity. How to keep alignment without becoming rigid. How to build structure without losing trust. How to grow Lean the same way it was started, by solving real problems that matter to real people.

Let's get into it.

Start Where It's Working

Scaling starts with energy. Not just need. That's the mistake most organizations make. They look for where things are broken and try to inject Lean as the fix. But when the pressure is highest, the appetite is lowest. People are defensive. The work is chaotic. And the trust required to experiment isn't there. That is not where you begin. You start where it's already working.

Look for the bright spots. The teams that leaned in early. The pockets where Lean was embraced, not imposed. Where leaders asked better questions. Where daily huddles became conversations, not checklists. Where problems surfaced without shame and people felt ownership to solve them. That is the ground to build on.

The reason is simple. Lean spreads by example. Not by mandate. When other teams see it in action, see how it made the work better, clearer, less frustrating, they pay attention. Not because they were told to. But because they want that too. That's how real scale starts. With curiosity. With proof. With the story told by the team doing the work.

And that proof needs to be visible. Not in slide decks. In real time. On the floor. In the language teams use. The metrics they track. The way they run their day. You are not looking for perfection. You are looking for belief. Belief that this is better than the way it was. That's what others will follow.

So before you plan the rollout, visit the places it's already growing. Watch how they work. Listen to how they talk. Learn what made it stick. Because when you start from strength, you scale with honesty. Not a pitch. Not a program. Just a better way to lead.

Name What's Working and Why

Success spreads faster when people understand it. Not just what happened, but why it worked. That's where most attempts to scale Lean lose traction. The results are visible, but the reasons behind them are not. Leaders try to copy the outcome without copying the behavior. That is how you get templates instead of thinking, rituals instead of routines, and surface change with no staying power.

Your job is to name it. Call out what the team did differently. How they made problems visible. How they responded. What conversations changed. What habits formed. What made it easier to lead. Not just the tool they used, but how they used it. Did they ask better questions in daily huddles? Did they set tighter expectations during shift changes? Did they simplify the way they tracked progress? Those details matter. Because those are the behaviors others can use.

And then say it plain. Not in Lean language. In team language. Make it something people can hear and repeat. The goal is not to explain the concept. It is to spark the "we could do that too" moment. That shift from watching to wanting. From audience to action. And the more grounded the example, the more likely that shift will happen.

This is not storytelling for motivation. This is pattern recognition for replication. When you name what worked and why, you create a path for others to follow without needing a roadmap. They don't have to guess what Lean looks like. They can see it. Feel it. Try it.

Watch for Slippage

Momentum is fragile. Especially in cultures that are still learning to trust change. One early success can light the fire. But it only takes a few missed signals to dim it. That's why the leader's job is not just to celebrate progress. It's to protect it.

Slippage does not start big. It starts with the little things. A board that used to be updated daily now lags by a week. A huddle that used to spark questions becomes a check-the-box routine. Metrics get gamed instead of challenged. Waste returns, not because people want it, but because no one noticed when the habits slipped. You have to notice.

> The goal is not to play Lean cop. The goal is to stay close enough to see when the culture begins to drift. When behaviors stop matching beliefs. When people nod along in meetings but don't act in the work. These are not signs of resistance. They are signs of habit loss. And habit loss is reversible if caught early.

This is where subtle leadership matters most. You step in without calling people out. You ask what changed. You ask what's getting in the way. You ask how you can help clear the path. And you do it fast. Because once slippage becomes the norm, the behavior that got you progress disappears, and with it, the results.

Staying power is not about pressure. It's about presence. Be close enough to see the cracks before they break. That is how you lead culture that sticks.

Interrupt the Drift

No culture holds its shape on its own. Even the best systems will drift if they are not anchored by steady, intentional leadership. This is not about bad people or failed training. It is about entropy. About the natural pull back toward old habits and shortcuts when no one is watching closely enough.

If you want habits to stick, you need to build in moments that catch the drift before it becomes a slide.

That means walking the floor with your eyes open. Listening in meetings not just for what's said but what's missing. It means noticing when the language changes, when teams stop saying "we improved this", and start saying "they told us to." That shift in tone is a warning. The behavior might still be there, but the belief behind it is fading. That is when you act.

You do not correct with blame. You correct with presence. You step in, ask why the drift happened, and bring the team back to the standard. Back to the habit that mattered. Not to punish, but to reconnect. Because people forget. Priorities stack up. New pressures show up. Drift is normal. Catching it is leadership.

Stickiness is not about being perfect. It is about not letting the culture slide when the spotlight moves on. It is about catching the little shifts before they become the new normal. That is how you make habits last. You notice. You act. You remind the system who it is.

Make It Hard to Unsee

Culture shifts when new thinking becomes the default. But that only happens when people see something they can't unsee. A truth so clear it changes how they look at the work from that point on. This is not about posters or slogans. It is about proof. Lived proof.

That moment when a frontline team sees waste in their own flow for the first time. When they track errors and realize most come from the same handoff. When a manager sees a metric shift because the team changed how they work instead of just working harder. These moments change more than process. They change perspective.

To make Lean stick, you need more of those moments. Not just training. Not just slides. Experiences. Hands-on, up close, undeniable proof that the tools work and the ideas matter. And once people see that, you do not need to sell Lean anymore. The work does it for you.

So design for it. Make the improvements visible. Share the story in the team's own words. Make it easy to connect what changed with why it mattered. That's how you turn behavior into belief. That's how you make the culture hard to undo.

Push Clarity to the Edges

As you scale, complexity creeps in. Layers add noise. Distance dulls intent. Leaders often try to fix that with more training, more slides, more messaging from the top. But real clarity is not what gets said in the boardroom. It is what gets repeated in a hallway, written on a whiteboard, or explained between teammates on a Tuesday.

If Lean is going to scale without losing its soul, people at the edge of the organization need to be able to explain what matters without translating. That means purpose must be plain. Standards must be simple. Expectations must travel without distortion. If you need a slide to explain the process, it is not clear enough. If the goal changes with every leader, it is not steady enough. If the values only live in posters, they are not real.

This is not about dumbing things down. It is about sharpening them. Distilling the essential truth of the work until anyone, anywhere, can pick it up and act with confidence. If you want consistency at scale, clarity is not a luxury. It is the lever. Push it all the way to the edge. That is how you grow without growing vague.

Default to Learning

Growth brings pressure. Pressure to perform. Pressure to replicate. Pressure to protect what worked. That pressure can quietly kill the curiosity that Lean depends on. When scale becomes the focus, experimentation starts to feel like a risk. Questions feel like a delay. Reflection gets replaced by rollout. That is when you lose the soul.

To keep Lean honest as you grow, leaders must create space to learn, not just centrally, but everywhere. That means protecting time for huddles. Asking what surprised people this week. Rewarding discovery, not just delivery. The best systems do not just ship processes. They ship feedback loops with them. They make learning part of the operating rhythm.

Defaulting to learning does not mean slowing down. It means speeding up the right way. When teams know that questions are not signs of failure but fuel for improvement, they build better systems faster. When leaders model reflection, they give permission to others to do the same. The most scalable cultures are not the ones with the most answers. They are the ones that never stop looking.

The Research Behind It

The theory behind *Default to Learning* comes from a blend of organizational psychology, behavioral science, and Lean thinking. At its core is the idea that **learning is not an outcome, it is a habit**. A system defaults to learning when it creates conditions where reflection, feedback, and experimentation are normalized instead of sidelined.

Psychologist Carol Dweck's work on *growth mindset* explains why this matters. Organizations that treat mistakes as data and value effort over perfection foster a mindset where people keep improving. That mindset becomes a cultural default when leaders reward curiosity and normalize uncertainty. Learning is not just tolerated, it is expected.

From a systems perspective, Lean thinkers like W. Edwards Deming and Taiichi Ohno emphasized the importance of feedback loops. Learning happens in real time, not in quarterly reviews. The system should make reflection easy, frequent, and visible. Every experiment, every problem solved, every failure caught early is part of the system's learning cycle.

When organizations fail to default to learning, they become brittle. They optimize for the present at the expense of adaptability. Success calcifies. Teams cling to what worked, even when the context changes. But in environments where learning is the norm, improvement compounds. People adapt, systems evolve, and innovation stays alive.

Leaders play the central role. If they model learning, asking questions, admitting what they do not know, and sharing what they are trying, others follow. This creates psychological safety, which is the hidden infrastructure behind every learning culture. Without it, teams stay quiet. With it, they speak up, test ideas, and push forward.

Defaulting to learning keeps Lean from becoming mechanical. It turns curiosity into a competitive advantage. It keeps people engaged. And it ensures that as you scale, you do not just replicate what you had, you build something that can keep growing on its own.

Design for Reflection

Reflection is where learning becomes insight. It is not about pausing for the sake of ceremony. It is about making space to ask what changed, what worked, and what should come next. Most teams skip this step because they are busy. But skipping reflection is like skipping sleep. You can do it for a while, but the cost compounds.

In strong Lean systems, reflection is designed into the work, not added on top. It shows up in huddles, after action reviews, and team debriefs. It is not about blame or status. It is about seeing clearly. The goal is not to document everything. The goal is to learn something worth using.

Reflection works best when it is routine, specific, and short. Routine keeps it from being forgotten. Specific keeps it grounded in the work. Short keeps it practical. You are not trying to write a report. You are trying to see the pattern so you can respond with purpose.

Leaders often miss the mark here. They ask, "What did we learn?" but do not make it safe to answer honestly. Or they reflect only when something breaks. But reflection should happen when things go right too. Especially then. That is how you build a culture that understands its own strengths and knows how to repeat them.

Designing for reflection means making it a habit that fits into the flow. It means being deliberate about when and how you look back. Not at the end of the quarter. In the moment. When the learning is fresh and the team can act on it. When reflection is built into the process, improvement speeds up. Clarity grows. And the team starts to think ahead instead of just looking back.

Build Triggers for New Habits

New behaviors do not stick because you explain them well. They stick because the system reminds people to use them. In Lean, those reminders are called triggers. They are small cues in the environment or the routine that prompt a better habit at the right time. You do not need more training. You need better triggers.

A trigger might be a question in a daily huddle: "What slowed us down yesterday?" It might be a step on a checklist: "Ask if the problem is system-driven." It might be a visual: a chart, a signal, a board that prompts thinking before doing. The key is timing. A good trigger shows up when the habit is needed, not when it is convenient.

This is where many Lean systems go soft. They launch the right practices, but the old cues remain. And when the pressure comes, people fall back on what they know. Not because they are resistant, but because the system does not help them remember. Habit wins. So if you want a new habit, you need to give it an edge.

> Make the trigger obvious. Make it tied to the real work. And make it easy to use without permission. The more friction there is, the faster it fades. This is not about posters or slogans. It is about practical cues that pull people into better thinking in real time.

When done right, triggers make good habits the default. They create consistency without having to demand it. And that is how Lean behavior scales. Not by force. By design.

Socialize the Win, Not the Hero

Culture grows through stories. But the kind of stories you tell determines the kind of culture you get. If you celebrate the hero, people wait for one. If you celebrate the win, people believe they can create one. That shift matters more than most leaders realize.

In early Lean efforts, it is tempting to highlight the person who stepped up. They worked late. They solved the issue. They carried the team. It makes a great story. But it sets the wrong precedent. It says success comes from effort, not from the system. And it teaches everyone else to wait for the next standout instead of becoming part of the solution.

The better way is to celebrate what changed. Not who changed it. Talk about how the team reduced rework, how they saw the waste, how they used the tools. Show how the process got better in a way others can learn from and repeat. If the story teaches a method, not a myth, it becomes fuel for cultural growth.

This is not about ignoring contributions. It is about redirecting attention to what others can copy. You want people to think, "We could do that," not, "They're just good at this." That shift creates momentum. It moves Lean from personality-driven to process-driven. And that is what makes it last.

Close the Loop with Ownership, Not Oversight

Sustained change does not come from better oversight. It comes from deeper ownership. When teams feel like they are being monitored, they protect themselves. When they feel like they are being trusted, they improve the work.

Leaders often try to make Lean stick by building checklists, reviews, and escalation paths. That might create accountability in the short term. But it does not build commitment. It does not build pride. It builds compliance. And compliance never sustains improvement.

The better move is to push decisions and reflection to the team. Ask them what's working. Ask what's not. Ask what they want to try next. Give them the data, give them the room, and let them run. If they miss the mark, coach them. Do not take it back. The goal is not perfection. It is progress they can own.

You will know this is working when updates sound like insight, not status. When teams bring you their next idea before you ask. When the habit of improvement shows up without the push. That is when Lean moves from a system you lead to a culture they live.

In Summary

Scaling does not mean copying. It means preserving what made Lean matter in the first place while giving it the room to grow. That takes discipline. That takes clarity. And that takes leaders who know the difference between spreading a method and keeping a promise. What makes Lean stick is not how many teams use the tools, but how deeply the habits take root. When people own the change, tell their own stories, and build systems they believe in, Lean becomes more than a program. It becomes the way work gets done. But belief needs support. It needs structure. That is where the tools come in. Not as checklists, but as thinking aids. Not to impress, but to expose the truth. That's what we will focus on next, the tools that help leaders see clearly, act wisely, and lead with intent. Let's get practical. Let's talk about tools and techniques that actually help.

Chapter Nine

Lean Tools and Techniques for Leaders

You do not need a belt color or a certification to lead with Lean. What you need are a few tools that help you see the work, support your team, and guide problem solving without adding complexity. This chapter is not about technical methods. It is about practical techniques leaders can use every day to reinforce the culture, improve performance, and stay close to what matters. These tools are simple, clear, and built to drive action. They do not require a rollout. They require repetition. What follows are the tools that make Lean real for leaders. Not in theory. In practice. Used often. Used well. And used with purpose.

Leader Standard Work

Leader standard work is not a checklist. It is how leaders create consistency in how they show up. Most leaders know what matters: coaching their teams, seeing the work, supporting problem solving, but the day gets filled with noise. Meetings stack up. Urgencies take over. What matters gets squeezed out. Leader standard work protects the time and space for the right behaviors. This tool matters because culture is not what you say. It is what you repeat. If you want problem solving, visibility, and accountability to be the norm, you have to show up for them. Not once. Not when there is time. Consistently.

Leader standard work is the routine that makes that happen. It builds the muscle. It sends the signal. It becomes what people expect.

Getting started is simple. Block time every day for three things: see the work, check the system, and coach the team. Start small. Maybe that means ten minutes with the visual board, ten minutes talking with the team, and ten minutes reviewing performance. Do not overdesign it. The power is in doing it regularly, not perfectly. You can write it on a whiteboard. Keep it in your notebook. Set calendar reminders if that helps. The point is not the format. The point is that it happens. When the team sees you consistently checking in, asking questions, and reinforcing what matters, the behavior sticks. If you stop, they notice that too.

You will know it is working when people start to anticipate the conversation. When they update the board before you arrive. When they come with their own observations. When they bring forward small problems without being asked. That is the shift. You are no longer pushing Lean. You are supporting it. The system starts to run because your habits set the pace.

> Leader standard work is not another task. It is how you protect the work that matters most. When done right, it anchors the culture you are trying to build. Not with announcements. With repetition. Not with tools. With presence. That is what makes it stick.

Leader standard work sets the rhythm. It keeps you focused on what matters. But showing up is not enough on its own. You need a way to connect with the team that is fast, clear, and consistent. That is where daily huddles come in. They are not meetings. They are checkpoints. A way to keep the work visible, surface issues early, and keep everyone aligned without slowing anyone down. Let's walk through how to use them the right way.

Daily Huddles

Daily huddles are not meetings. They are short, structured checkpoints that keep teams aligned, make problems visible, and reinforce ownership. Most leaders say communication matters. Huddles are how you prove it. They are fast, focused, and predictable. They create space to talk about the work while the work is happening. Not in a report. Not at the end of the month. Right now.

Huddles matter because they keep the team connected to the process and to each other. They shift the conversation from updates to action. They give people a place to call out what is in the way and what needs support. And they make it clear that solving problems is not a side task. It is part of the work.

Getting started is simple. Pick a consistent time. Pick a consistent place. Stand up. Keep it under ten minutes. Talk about three things. What did we complete? What are we working on today? What is getting in the way? That is enough. You are not reviewing metrics or tracking every task. You are looking for flow. You are looking for blockers. You are reinforcing that people own the work and the problems that come with it. Use a board or a whiteboard if you want to make it visual. Let the team lead it. Your job is to show up, listen, and support. If something needs to be solved outside the huddle, take it offline. The point is not to fix everything in the moment. The point is to stay connected and make sure the team has what it needs to move forward.

You will know it is working when people start coming prepared. When blockers are raised early and solved before they grow. When updates are focused, and ownership starts to shift from the leader to the team. You will also know it is working when the huddle runs without you and still adds value. That is the sign of trust and rhythm taking hold.

Daily huddles are not another meeting on the calendar. They are a leadership habit. They set the tone for the day and build the discipline to stay close to the work. Do them well and do them often. They will tell you what is working, what is stuck, and what your team needs from you. No guesswork. Just visibility. Every day.

Daily huddles keep the team aligned, but they only work if the work is visible. You cannot manage what you cannot see. You cannot improve what stays hidden. That is where visual management comes in. It takes the work, the goals, and the problems and puts them where everyone can see them. No chasing. No guessing. Just clear signals that keep people focused and informed. Let's walk through what that looks like when it is done right.

Visual Management

Visual management makes the work visible. That includes the flow of the work, the status of the work, the goals tied to the work, and the problems blocking the work. You are not making a dashboard. You are creating shared awareness. When people can see what is happening, they do not have to ask. When leaders can see where things stand, they do not have to chase. It replaces guessing with clarity.

This matters because teams lose time and energy when they have to dig for answers. If no one knows what is in progress, what is waiting, or what is blocked, then every handoff becomes a conversation. Every check-in becomes a search. Visual management clears the fog. It makes the current state obvious so people can act faster and smarter. It also keeps leaders honest. You cannot fix what you are not willing to look at. Getting started is simple. Start where the work happens. Pick one board. Start tracking a few basic things. What is being worked on, what is done, what is stuck. You do not need software. You need clarity. Use sticky notes, magnets, or printed cards. You are not building a report. You are building a conversation. The board should tell the story without someone needing to explain it. Keep the format simple. Make it something the team can update without asking. Add visual signals for problems. That could be red dots, blocked tags, or handwritten notes. The key is to make sure the team owns the board. If the leader is the only one touching it, it is a tool for reporting. When the team uses it to guide their work, it becomes a tool for learning.

You will know it is working when you can walk up to the board and understand the status of the work in thirty seconds. You will know it is working when people start talking about what is on the board without being prompted. You will know it is working when someone walks by, points to a problem, and says, we need to fix that. That is the shift. The work is no longer hidden. It is visible, shared, and owned.

Visual management is not decoration. It is not Lean theater. It is a habit that helps teams stay aligned and take action without waiting for permission. If you want better conversations, faster decisions, and fewer surprises, start by making the work visible. Let the team see what they are solving. Let the leader see what matters. Let the problems show up where they belong. Out in the open. Where they can be fixed.

Leader Roadmap for Standing Up, Assessing, and Maintaining Visual Management

Step 1: Stand it up

Start where the work happens. Do not start with a template. Start with the team. Ask one question. What do we need to see every day to know where things stand? That question sets the foundation. Then build the board around the answers. The goal is not design. The goal is clarity.

Pick the basics. What is being worked on? What is done? What is blocked? Add a space for daily metrics or goals if it helps the team stay focused. Keep the layout simple. Use a whiteboard, sticky notes, printed cards, or magnets. If it takes more than ten seconds to update, it will not last.

Make the board part of the work. Not a project. Not a report. If the team cannot update it without you, it is not visual management. It is tracking. That is not the same thing.

Step 2: Assess how it is working

After a few days, step back and ask five questions:

1. Can I walk up and understand what is happening in thirty seconds

2. Are problems showing up on the board, or just progress

3. Is the team using the board during daily huddles

4. Are updates happening live, or is someone catching it up later

5. Is the board prompting conversations and action

If the answer is no to most of these, it is not visual management. It is decoration. Fix it now before it becomes background noise. Do not wait for a monthly review. Check weekly. Walk the floor. Watch how people interact with the board. Ask what has changed. Ask what is missing. Adjust with the team. Keep it real.

Step 3: Maintain and improve it

Consistency beats polish. Make sure the board is updated daily. That is not a task. That is a discipline. It keeps the team engaged and keeps the work honest. If it is empty or outdated, it sends the message that the work does not matter.

Review the layout every quarter. Ask the team what is working and what is not. Add or remove sections as needed. The board should evolve as the process improves. If the work changes but the board stays the same, it will lose its value.

Recognize the behavior, not the tool. Do not compliment the board. Call out the team for raising a blocker or fixing something that showed up. That keeps the focus where it belongs. On ownership and action.

Final check

You will know visual management is working when the board leads the conversation instead of the meeting agenda. When someone walks by, points to a problem, and starts the fix. When updates happen without being asked. That is when it is no longer a tool. It is a habit. Keep it simple. Keep it visible. Keep it owned by the team. That is how leaders make visual management work. Not once. Every day. Repeated. Backed by presence. Driven by purpose. Done right, it does not just show the work. It changes it.

Visual management helps you see the work at a glance, but boards and charts only tell part of the story. To really understand what is happening, you have to go to the source. You have to see it for yourself. That is where go see comes in. It is not a walk through. It is not a drive by. It is how leaders stay grounded in reality by watching the work, asking questions, and listening without a filter. Let's break down what that looks like when it is done with purpose.

Go See

Go see means you do not lead from a distance. You go to where the work is happening. You look at it with your own eyes. You ask questions. You listen. You stay present long enough to see what is real, not just what is reported. This is not a walk through. It is not a scheduled appearance. It is how leaders stay grounded in the actual work, not the version of the work they get in updates or presentations. This matters because no board, no system, and no meeting will ever show you what real observation can. If you are not seeing the process with your own eyes, you are leading through assumption. That is where gaps live. That is where waste hides. Go see pulls you out of the office and puts you back in the environment where value is created. It shows the truth. Not the story. The truth.

Getting started is simple. Block time each week to be in the work area. Go without an agenda. Watch the flow. Look for delays. Look for confusion. Look for extra steps. Ask questions like, what makes this harder than it should be, or, what slows you down most often. Then listen. Do not offer solutions. Do not start fixing. Just observe and learn.

Bring a notebook. Write down what you see. Listen for patterns. When the same issues show up across different teams or shifts, you are not dealing with opinion. You are seeing signals. And those signals guide your next step. You are not there to audit. You are there to understand.

You will know it is working when people stop performing and start showing you what is real. When they point out problems instead of hiding them. When you no longer have to ask where things stand because you can see it yourself. You will also know it is working when your questions start to shape how others see their own process. That is the shift. You stop leading through answers. You start leading through presence.

> Go see is not a task. It is a habit. It builds trust. It shows respect. It keeps your decisions rooted in reality. The longer you stay disconnected from the work, the easier it becomes to miss what matters. Go see fixes that. One visit at a time. Quiet. Consistent. Intentional. It changes how you lead. Because it changes what you see.

How to Get Started with Effective Go See

If you want to make go see part of how you lead, do not treat it like an event. Treat it like a habit. You are not adding a task. You are removing guesswork. What follows is a clear, repeatable way to get started. No setup. No rollout. Just presence and discipline.

Step 1: Schedule it like it matters

Block time on your calendar every week. Pick a consistent time and protect it. Start with thirty minutes. If you do not make space for it, the noise will fill it. This is not a surprise visit. It is a leadership practice. Show up often enough that your presence becomes normal.

Step 2: Pick a process, not a person

You are not visiting a team member. You are observing a process. That could be how work is prepared, handed off, reviewed, or completed. Do not float. Pick something specific. Go to the location where that part of the work happens. This gives the visit focus without needing a script.

Step 3: Watch without interrupting

Stand back. Watch the flow. Do not start with questions. Let the work unfold. Look for delays, handoffs, confusion, or extra steps. Watch how people respond when problems happen. You are not there to find fault. You are there to learn what the work really looks like.

Step 4: Ask open questions

After observing, ask questions that uncover friction. What part of this is harder than it should be? What slows you down? What would you change if you could? Do not try to solve it. Just listen. Write down what they say. If more than one person gives you the same answer, pay attention. That is a signal.

Step 5: Reflect, do not react

When the visit is done, go back and review your notes. Do not jump into action. Look for patterns across different visits. Which problems keep showing up? Where are the gaps between how the process is supposed to work and how it actually runs? These gaps are where your next support should go.

Step 6: Follow up without taking over

Go back to the team later and ask what they have done since your last visit. Not as a test. As a signal that their input matters. Offer support if needed. Ask if anything has improved. This shows respect without control. The team owns the work. You own the follow through.

You will know go see is working when the team no longer adjusts their behavior when you show up. When people bring problems to you before you ask. When you stop being surprised by what is happening in your own operation. When your questions change the way others look at the work. Go see is not about visibility. It is about clarity. And clarity is what strong leadership is built on.

Go see keeps leaders grounded in the reality of the work, but seeing the problem is not enough. You have to help others work through it. That does not mean solving it for them. It means asking the kind of questions that lead to ownership, action, and better thinking. That is where problem solving coaching comes in. It is not a method. It is a leadership habit. Let's break down how to use it with purpose.

Problem Solving Coaching

Problem solving coaching is how leaders build capability without taking control. You are not handing out answers. You are guiding people to think clearly, take action, and learn from what happens. This is how you develop teams that fix what is broken instead of waiting for direction This matters because too many problems get escalated not because they are complex, but because people do not know how to work through them. Coaching fills that gap. It gives the team a way to slow down their thinking just enough to focus. You are not giving them a template. You are giving them space and direction. Start with five simple questions:

1. What is the problem?

2. What is causing it?

3. What have you tried?

4. What happened?

5. What will you do next?

That is it. Do not turn this into a checklist. These questions are not a tool. They are a mindset. You ask them in conversation. You ask them in huddles. You ask them during go see. You ask them any time someone is stuck or spinning. They create clarity. They cut through noise.

Getting started is easy. Write the five questions down. Use them once a day. Ask them when someone brings you a problem. Ask them when someone shares an idea. Ask them when something failed. The goal is not to be clever. The goal is to help the team think. You are not challenging them. You are coaching them to slow down just enough to see what matters.

You will know it is working when people start using the questions on their own. When they come to you already thinking through what they have tried and what they are going to do next. When problem solving becomes expected instead of exceptional. That is the shift. The questions become part of the way the team works.

> Problem solving coaching is not about having the answer. It is about building teams that know how to get to one. You do not need a whiteboard. You need presence. You do not need to fix it. You need to stay curious. That is what keeps problem solving alive. Not more training. Better questions. Repeated often. Backed by action. Quiet leadership that shows up in how you think, not what you say.

Coaching helps teams slow down their thinking, but once a problem is clear, they need a way to find what is actually causing it. Most teams stop too early. They fix the symptom and move on. That creates a cycle of rework, frustration, and wasted effort. The Five Whys stops that. It forces the conversation below the surface so the real cause can be seen and fixed. Let's get into how it works and how to use it the right way.

The Five Whys for Leaders

The Five Whys is the simplest and most effective root cause tool leaders can use. You ask why something happened. Then you ask why again. You do this five times or until you hit the real cause. You do not guess. You do not accept the first answer. You keep digging until the answer is something the team can control and fix. This matters because most organizations fix the symptom. A form was wrong, so they change the form. A task was late, so they remind someone to be faster. That is not problem solving. That is surface correction. The issue comes back because the cause was never removed. The Five Whys pushes past that. It turns attention to the system, not just the people.

To get started, pick one issue that matters. Something recent. Something that caused confusion, delay, or rework. Then write down what happened. Start with the outcome. From there, ask why it happened. Keep going until the answer points to a process failure, not a person. If the answer is blame, keep going. If the answer is vague, keep going. You are looking for something that can be changed.

Write each why and each answer on a whiteboard or piece of paper. Use the team's words. Do not wordsmith. Do not fix while you are diagnosing. Just get to the bottom. Once you get to a root cause, stop. That is your target for improvement. Then act.

You will know it is working when teams start asking why without being told. When people hesitate to fix a problem until they understand it. When blame drops out of the conversation and system thinking takes its place. You will also know it is working when problems stop coming back.

The Five Whys is not a worksheet. It is a habit. When used well, it saves hours of rework and endless frustration. You are not teaching analysis. You are building discipline. Ask why. Then ask it again. Every time. Until you get to something that can be fixed and stays fixed. That is what root cause looks like. Simple. Sharp. Repeatable. And built into the way your team thinks.

The Five Whys helps teams get to the root of a single problem, but sometimes the challenge is bigger. More steps. More people. More moving parts. When that happens, teams need a simple way to structure the thinking so they do not get lost in noise or skip ahead to solutions. That is where A3 thinking comes in. It is not a template. It is a way to think clearly, focus on what matters, and drive improvement with discipline.

A3 Thinking

A3 thinking is how you organize a problem so the thinking stays clear, the action stays focused, and the team stays aligned. It is not a form. It is a way to think through a problem without losing the thread. One page. One issue. One path from problem to result. This matters because teams often talk in circles. People have different versions of the problem. One group is solving the symptom. Another group is guessing. Leaders lose patience, teams lose focus, and nothing sticks. A3 thinking fixes that. It puts the facts, the causes, the target, and the next step in one place. Everyone sees the same thing. Everyone moves in the same direction.

To get started, pick a real problem. One that affects the team and the process. Not a complaint. Not a suggestion box item. Something tied to flow, quality, or delivery. Use the A3 format to write down four things:

1. What is happening?

2. Why it matters?

3. What is causing it?

4. What we are doing about it?

Use short phrases. Stay away from buzzwords. Include only what the team needs to move. Keep it on one page. If you need a deck to explain the A3, it is not working. Let the team write it. Coach them to be specific. Review it together. Use it to drive action, not discussion. The A3 should move with the problem. As you test countermeasures and learn what works, update it. That turns it into a record of how the team solved something real.

You will know it is working when teams stay on track without being pushed. When they can explain what is happening and what they are doing about it in thirty seconds. When decisions are based on shared understanding, not opinion. A3 thinking builds that discipline.

This is not documentation. It is focus. The paper does not solve the problem. The team does. The A3 just keeps the path clear. One problem. One team. One result that sticks. That is what makes it worth using. Not for show. For progress.

How to Coach A3 Thinking as a Leader

If you want teams to get better at solving problems, you do not fill out the A3 for them. You coach the thinking behind it. A3 is not a tool for compliance. It is a tool for clarity. Your job is not to review the page. Your job is to shape how the team sees the problem, challenges their own thinking, and follows through with action. Here is how to do that the right way.

Step 1: Do not start with the form

Start with the conversation. Ask what problem they are working on and why it matters. If they cannot explain it in a sentence, they are not ready to write it down. Do not let them start with countermeasures. If the cause is not clear, the fix will not hold. You are coaching the thinking, not the formatting.

Step 2: Challenge the problem definition

Ask, is this a symptom or the real problem? What is the evidence? Who is impacted and how often? Push for specifics. If the problem is vague, the rest of the A3 will fall apart. You are not being difficult. You are keeping the team honest. If they get this part right, the rest is easier.

Step 3: Test the cause thinking

Ask, what do you think is causing it? What have you seen that points to that? What else could it be? Look for assumptions. If the team cannot explain how the cause leads to the effect, they are still guessing. Tell them to walk the process again. Ask for data. Get them to pause before they act. This is where most A3s fall short. Fixing the wrong thing is worse than doing nothing.

Step 4: Review the target condition

Ask, what does success look like? How will you know it is better? What does better mean in numbers or behavior? You are not asking for perfection. You are asking for a clear end state. Something they can measure or see. If there is no target, there is no learning. There is just motion.

Step 5: Focus the countermeasures

Ask, what will you try? What do you expect it to change? What are the risks? Push them to test one change at a time. If they stack five ideas together, they will not know what worked. Remind them that countermeasures are not permanent. They are tested. If it works, they can lock it in. If not, they learn something and try again.

Step 6: Follow up on the result

Ask, what happened? Did it solve the problem? What did you learn? If the answer is that the fix worked, ask how they know. If it failed, ask what they would do differently next time. Never let the conversation end with, we think it is better. Better needs evidence. This is not a pass or fail test. It is a cycle.

You will know the coaching is working when the team brings you A3s with thinking behind them, not just boxes filled in. When the problem is sharp, the cause is tested, and the fix is measured. When they update the A3 after learning something instead of trying to get it signed off. That is the shift. You are not reviewing their work. You are building their thinking. That is what lasts.

Do not make it formal. Make it frequent. Coach in the moment. Challenge with respect. Reward the process, not just the result. That is how you turn the A3 from a tool into a habit. And that is what makes the team stronger. Every time they solve a real problem with real thinking, the work gets better. So do they. And so do you.

A3 thinking gives structure to problem solving, but once the process improves, you need a way to lock it in. If the team makes progress but everyone keeps doing it their own way, the improvement fades. That is where standard work comes in. It does not slow the team down. It keeps the progress from slipping. Let's get into how leaders use it to build stability, set a baseline, and make future improvement possible.

Standard Work

Standard work is the best known way to complete a task that is clear, repeatable, and stable. It captures the method that works so everyone starts from the same place. This is not a script. This is not about control. It is about making sure people do not have to figure it out every time. When work is stable, problems are easier to see and easier to fix. This matters because a lot of teams solve problems, but they do not hold the gain. One person makes an improvement, but the next person does it their own way. The variation brings the waste right back. Standard work protects the improvement. It is the anchor. Without it, you are constantly solving the same issue over and over.

To get started, find a process that runs often and touches multiple people. Something with handoffs, timing, or repeatable tasks. Watch the best version of the process. See what actually works. Then write it down. Keep it short. Keep it clear. Use checklists, visuals, or simple steps. The goal is not to make it perfect. The goal is to make it consistent.

Work with the team to define it. Do not write it in a room by yourself. Ask what steps matter most. Ask where things usually break down. Ask what would make training easier. Then write what you all agree works best right now. This becomes the baseline. Not the ceiling. You can still improve it. But you are no longer reinventing the wheel every time. Review it regularly. Ask the team if it still works. Watch the process again. When you improve it, update the standard. That is how standard work and continuous improvement go together. You stabilize the process. You learn. You adjust. Then you stabilize again.

You will know it is working when training is faster, errors drop, and the team calls out when something breaks from the standard. You will know it is working when problems stand out because the process is clear. You are not guessing what went wrong. You are watching for deviation. That gives you control without being controlling.

> Standard work is not about forcing people to be the same. It is about giving the team a clear, shared way to succeed. It is the baseline that makes learning possible and improvement sustainable. Done right, it removes confusion, reduces frustration, and protects the progress you already earned. Not for documentation. For discipline. So the work stays strong even when no one is watching.

Back in my day. An author reflection.

Back in my day, I was working with a vendor that handled title releases for banks that finance cars. Their job was to confirm that a car loan had been paid off, release the lien, and send the title to the right place. It sounds simple. It was not. Every bank had a different system. Every state had different rules. Some titles were electronic. Some were not. Some required a physical stamp. Some needed confirmation from state systems that updated once a week. The result was constant chaos.

The team handling the work was sharp. They knew the details. They cared about the outcome. But every rep had their own way of getting it done. One would wait to batch them. One would check a different database first. One liked to sort by lender. Another would go by state. They were all trying to be efficient, but it made training impossible and errors unpredictable. When something broke, no one could explain why. Everyone said they followed the process. The truth was there was no process.

We worked with them to define the best known way. Not the perfect way. The one that balanced speed, accuracy, and the mess of rules they had to work through. We mapped it out. We tested it. We asked the team what felt repeatable and what did not. Then we wrote it down. Three steps. One check. One handoff. That became the standard.

It did not fix every problem. But it gave them a baseline. New reps were trained faster. Errors dropped. Questions shifted from "what happened" to "what changed." That was the real win. Once the process was stable, they could see where the issues really lived. Before that, it was just noise.

Standard work did not slow them down. It gave them control. And once they had control, improvement was possible. That is why it matters. Not because it looks clean. Because it keeps the work from falling apart when things get messy.

Standard work brings stability to how tasks are done, but stability is not enough when work is piling up, stuck in queues, or scattered across systems. You need a way to manage the flow of that work as it moves through the process. That is where visual flow control comes in. Often called Kanban, this is not a software tool or a Lean label. It is a practical way to see what is in motion, what is waiting, and what needs help. Let's walk through how leaders use it to create focus, limit chaos, and improve delivery.

Visual Flow Control (Kanban)

Kanban is a simple way to see the flow of work. It shows what is being worked on, what is waiting, and what is done. That is it. Nothing fancy. Just a clear picture of where the work stands and where it is getting stuck. It works because you do not have to guess. You do not have to ask. You can walk up and see what is moving and what is not. This matters because most teams are overloaded and do not know it. Everything is urgent. Everything is in motion. But no one can see how much is truly in play or where the real bottlenecks are. Kanban makes the invisible visible. When the work is out in the open, you can prioritize it. You can focus it. You can manage it.

To get started, build a board with three basic columns. To do. Doing. Done. Start there. Write each task or item on a card. Use sticky notes, index cards, magnets, or whatever makes it easy to move. Add names or owners if it helps. Keep it simple. This is not project management. This is flow management. Once the board is up, start limiting how much can be in progress at once. That is the part most leaders skip. But it is the part that makes it work. If everything is being worked on, nothing is getting finished. Set a limit. Three tasks per person. Five cards in the doing column. Whatever fits your team. Stick to it. When something is done, then you pull the next item. Not before.

Use the board in daily huddles. Look at what is moving. Talk about what is stuck. Ask why things are not getting finished. You are not there to police. You are there to help the team stay focused. The board is not a report. It is a mirror. It shows how the work is flowing...or not.

You will know it is working when the team starts pulling their own work instead of waiting to be assigned. When they talk about flow instead of just volume. When work gets done faster because less is in motion. You will also know it is working when the board becomes part of the conversation, not just a background piece.

> Kanban is not a system you install. It is a way to bring order to the noise. It gives the team and the leader a shared view of reality. Not what is planned. Not what is expected. What is actually happening. That is what makes it powerful. It is visual. It is flexible. And when used right, it creates the focus most teams are missing. Not more meetings. More flow. Less friction. Better outcomes. All on one board.

Visual flow tools like Kanban help teams see the work and manage what is in motion, but seeing the flow is not the same as pacing it. Most teams push work forward as fast as possible or wait until it stacks up. Neither one creates stability. That is where takt time comes in. It sets the rhythm. It gives the team a steady beat to match their effort to demand. This is not about speed. It is about balance. Let's walk through how leaders use takt time to create flow that is steady, not chaotic.

Takt Time

Takt time is the pace of work needed to meet customer demand without overproducing or falling behind. It sets the rhythm. Not how fast you can go. How fast you should go to stay balanced. You are not chasing speed. You are setting flow. That flow keeps the team focused, the workload steady, and the customer satisfied. This matters because most teams move in spikes. They do too much at once, burn out, then stall. Or they wait until the work piles up, then scramble. Takt time fixes that. It tells you how often something needs to be completed based on how much time you have and what the customer expects. It gives the process a beat. Just like music. Without it, everything feels off.

To get started, calculate it. Take the total available work time and divide it by the number of units needed. That is your takt time. If you have 400 minutes in a day and the customer needs 100 approvals, the takt time is 4 minutes. That means one approval every 4 minutes keeps you on track. More than that, and you fall behind. Less than that, and you are likely creating waste or overworking the team. Once you know your takt time, compare it to the actual cycle time. That is the time it takes to do the task today. If your cycle time is longer than your takt time, you need to remove waste or rebalance the work. If it is much shorter, you may be building ahead or overprocessing. Either one causes problems downstream.

You do not need a timer on the wall. You just need awareness. Use the number to check whether the process is paced to meet demand. Talk about it during huddles. Use it when planning staffing. Use it when someone asks why the work feels rushed or stalled. Takt time gives you a neutral reference point. It is not opinion. It is math.

You will know it is working when the team starts managing workload based on flow, not pressure. When the pace is sustainable. When the team can focus without feeling like everything is urgent. You will also know it is working when you stop building inventory just to look busy and start delivering exactly what is needed, when it is needed.

Takt time is not a speed target. It is a balance point. It keeps the system stable, the team calm, and the customer satisfied. Most work falls apart when pacing is ignored. Takt time brings that rhythm back. One task. One team. One steady beat that everyone can follow.

How to Get Started with Takt Time as a Leader

Takt time is not a tool for specialists. It is a leadership tool for setting pace, finding balance, and calling out when the work is misaligned with demand. You do not need a workshop. You need to know how to do the math, ask the right questions, and guide the team toward better flow. Here is how to get started.

Step 1: Pick one process tied to demand

Do not overthink it. Choose one repeatable task that has a clear customer expectation. Something like approvals per day, calls handled per shift, tickets resolved per week. The key is that it repeats and the demand is steady enough to make the math meaningful.

Step 2: Calculate your available work time

Take the total time your team has to do the work. Subtract breaks, meetings, and anything that takes time away from the task. If your team works eight hours and has one hour of meetings and breaks, you have seven hours left. That is 420 minutes of available work time.

Step 3: Divide by customer demand

Now divide that available time by how many units of work the customer needs in that same window. If the customer needs 210 approvals in a day, and you have 420 minutes available, then 420 divided by 210 equals 2. Your takt time is 2 minutes per approval. That is the pace you need to stay on track. Not faster. Not slower.

Step 4: Compare it to your actual cycle time

Cycle time is how long it actually takes to complete one unit of work. Time it. Do not guess. If your current cycle time is 5 minutes and your takt time is 2 minutes, you are not keeping up. If your cycle time is 1 minute, you are ahead….but at what cost? Look for overload or overproduction. The goal is to match, not outpace.

Step 5: Use takt time to guide decisions

Once you know your takt time, use it. Ask if the team is paced to meet it. Ask how much variation there is. Ask what breaks the rhythm. Use it to adjust staffing, prioritize tasks, and rebalance when things shift. Takt time gives you a reference point that is based on demand, not pressure.

Step 6: Teach the team to use it

Share the number. Explain what it means. Show how it connects to the customer. Let them track how close they are to the pace. This is not about micro-tracking. It is about awareness. Once the team understands takt time, they can manage themselves with more focus and less chaos.

You will know it is working when the team starts talking about pacing instead of pushing. When they flag problems that slow the flow. When workload feels steady and aligned with what the customer needs. You will know it is working when the process runs smoother, not faster, and the team stays engaged without burning out.

Takt time is not about pushing people. It is about building systems that run with rhythm and purpose. When leaders bring that rhythm into the work, flow follows. And once flow takes hold, everything gets easier to manage. Every process has a beat. Takt time helps you find it. Then lead with it.

Takt time helps you pace the work. It shows when the system is off rhythm. But when things are breaking down and you have limited time or resources, you need to know where to start. That is where Pareto charts come in. They show what problems are doing the most damage. You do not need to fix everything. You need to fix the right things. Let's walk through how leaders use Pareto charts to focus effort where it actually moves the needle.

Pareto Charts

Pareto charts show you where to focus. Not where the noise is. Where the impact is. They take a list of problems and rank them from most frequent to least. That is it. Nothing complicated. Just a clear view of which issues are costing you the most and which ones can wait. This matters because most teams spend too much time chasing small problems. They try to fix everything at once. That spreads people thin and delivers almost nothing. A Pareto chart stops that. It brings focus. It tells the truth. It makes it clear that most of your problems are coming from a few causes.

To get started, pick a category. Maybe it is customer complaints, defects, delays, or system failures. Track the number of times each one happens over a set period. Then put that data in a simple bar chart. The tallest bar goes first. The rest follow in order. Add a line to show cumulative impact if you want, but you do not need it to get value. Once it is up, look for the break point. That is where the chart drops off. Most of the time, you will see that two or three issues are driving the majority of the pain. That is where you focus. Not because the others do not matter. But because these matter more. This is how you protect your team's energy. You solve what hits the hardest first.

Use the chart to guide action. Do not let it become wallpaper. Talk about it during huddles. Ask what is being done to address the top issue. Ask what will change when it is solved. Ask what the team needs to move it forward. When the top issue improves, update the chart and shift focus to the next.

You will know it is working when improvement conversations start with facts instead of opinions. When teams stop picking easy fixes and start picking the most important ones. When leaders stop asking for everything and start asking for the right thing. You will also know it is working when the same issue does not keep coming back because you solved what caused it.

> Pareto charts do not fix problems. They tell you where to look. They bring discipline to the chaos and turn random effort into targeted action. You do not need more time. You need better focus. And the Pareto chart gives it to you. Every time. Clear. Prioritized. Proven.

Once you know where to focus using a Pareto chart, the next step is choosing what to do about it. Most teams generate a long list of ideas. Some are easy. Some are heavy lifts. Without a way to sort them, they either do nothing or do too much. That is where the impact versus effort matrix comes in. It gives the team a fast, visual way to decide what is worth doing now and what can wait. Let's walk through how leaders use it to drive action without draining the team.

Impact versus Effort Matrix

The impact versus effort matrix is a simple way to prioritize improvement ideas. It forces the team to step back and ask two questions. How much effort does this take. How much impact will it have. That is it. You plot each idea on a grid. High or low effort. High or low impact. The goal is to make the next step obvious. This matters because most teams treat all ideas the same. They chase the ones that sound exciting or come from the loudest voice. That creates waste and burnout. The matrix fixes that. It points you to the ideas that move the needle without draining the team. Quick wins. High leverage. Low drag.

To get started, gather the team and list out every possible improvement related to a problem you are trying to solve. Write each one on a sticky note or virtual card. Then draw a two by two grid. One side is effort. The other is impact. Place each idea based on where the team believes it fits. Do not get stuck in debate. The goal is alignment, not precision. Once they are placed, you will see four quadrants. High impact and low effort is your priority. Do those first. They build momentum. Low impact and high effort goes last. Or not at all. High impact and high effort becomes your next wave. Low impact and low effort can be handled if capacity allows. This is how you keep the work focused.

Use the matrix to narrow the list. Do not try to fix everything. Pick one or two actions. Execute them. Track what changes. Then come back to the board and pick the next round. Keep it active. Keep it honest. When the team sees that ideas lead to action and that effort is respected, they stay engaged.

You will know it is working when teams stop asking for permission to try and start asking where to focus. When the loudest idea is not the first one chosen. When energy is spent on the work that matters most. You will also know it is working when people stop saying they are too busy and start saying, we can do this one.

The impact versus effort matrix is not a form. It is a decision tool. It gives leaders and teams a clear way to say yes to the right things and no to the rest. That is how you drive improvement that lasts. Focused. Practical. Balanced. And done on purpose. Every time.

In Summary

You do not need a title or a belt color to use Lean tools. You need rhythm. You need presence. You need the discipline to keep showing up for what matters. This chapter walked through the daily habits that help leaders stay close to the work and support teams without adding complexity. Leader standard work protects the right behaviors. Huddles keep the team aligned. Visual boards make the work clear. Go see brings leaders back to what is real. Coaching sharpens thinking. The Five Whys and A3 keep problem solving focused. Standard work holds the gain. Kanban creates flow. Takt time sets the pace. Pareto charts bring focus. The impact versus effort matrix keeps the team grounded in what is worth doing now. These are not advanced tools. They are leadership habits. When used well, they create structure without noise and clarity without pressure.

But the work does not stop there. These habits help you lead. They help you listen. But to solve what matters most, you need to know how to read the signals. That is where the seven quality tools come in. Simple, visual, and built to cut through noise. You do not need to master statistics. You just need to understand what each tool shows and how to act on it. These tools are not technical. They are practical. And they help leaders know where the problem lives, how big it is, and what needs to happen next. Let's get into how to use them the right way. With purpose. With clarity. Without overthinking it.

Chapter Ten

Leading with the Other Quality Tools

Most quality tools were not designed for experts. They were designed to help people see the problem. That is still the point. These tools are not about graphs. They are not about templates. They are not about impressing anyone. They are about giving leaders and teams a simple way to move from guessing to knowing. From reacting to solving.

This chapter is not about how to build the tools. You do not need a tutorial. You need to know when to use them, what they are telling you, and what to do next. That is where most training goes off track. It teaches people how to make a chart, but not how to use it to lead. That is the gap we are going to close here.

Each of the seven tools in this chapter does one job. Each one helps you see something that is usually missed. Some show where the problem is. Some show how big it is. Some help you track if your fix is working. None of them *solve the issue*. But they all help you ask better questions and take better action. That is their value.

You are not a statistician. You are a leader. Your job is not to crunch the numbers. Your job is to use the right tool to surface the truth and support the team as they act on it. You do not need to know every function in Excel. You need to know what to look for and what to ask when you see it.

We will go one at a time. We will keep it practical. For each tool, we will walk through three things. When to use it. What to look for. And how to respond. No theory. Just grounded, real-time leadership. These are not add-ons. They are part of how strong Lean systems stay honest and focused.

Let's get into the first one. The one that makes the pattern obvious when it is hiding in plain sight. The one that shows you what is happening over time. Let's start with the run chart.

Run Chart

What It Tells You

A run chart shows you how something is behaving over time. That could be response times, approval volume, or cycle time, or anything that happens in a sequence. It puts the data on a simple line graph and lets you see the pattern. You are not looking for a spike or a dip. You are looking for a rhythm. A run chart tells you if the process is stable, drifting, or sending up a signal.

This is not about whether the number is high or low. It is about whether the system is behaving the way it should. Is it predictable? Is it consistent? Are we seeing the same pattern over and over or are we getting surprised? The chart does not give you the answer. It tells you what question to ask next. That is what makes it powerful. It pulls you out of reacting to a single number and into leading with pattern recognition. You are not watching for performance. You are watching for behavior.

When to Use It

Use a run chart when you need to understand the trend behind the noise. Not the best day. Not the worst day. The actual flow of the system. Run charts work best when you are watching one metric over time and you want to know if the process is steady or slipping. They are useful early in an improvement effort, when you are trying to understand what normal looks like. They are just as useful later, when you are checking if the new process is holding.

If you are in a huddle and someone says "we hit our number yesterday," this is how you ask, "but what does the trend say?" Run charts are also helpful when the pressure is on and leaders want to know if something is fixed. This chart does not tell you if the metric is good. It tells you if the fix worked. That is the difference.

LEADING WITH THE OTHER QUALITY TOOLS

Use it when teams are stuck in reactive mode. Use it when the noise is louder than the pattern. Use it when people are chasing exceptions and missing the signal. A run chart brings the conversation back to process.

What to Watch For

Look for sudden shifts. If the line moves and stays there, something in the system changed. That is not luck. That is signal. Ask what changed and whether the process was adjusted or just stretched. Look for long runs above or below the median. That means the system is drifting. Not a spike. A slide. Something that feels normal until the results get too far out to recover.

Also watch for tight patterns that suddenly get noisy. That is usually a sign the process is breaking down. Not a single failure. A weakening of the system. A team doing extra to keep the number in range but burning out behind the scenes. That kind of change shows up in the pattern before it shows up in the people.

Do not get distracted by one good point. Do not overreact to one bad one. Let the chart tell you the story of what is happening across time. If the pattern shifts, ask why. If it holds, ask what is keeping it steady. If it looks random, ask what the team is relying on to get through the day. These questions matter more than the chart itself. They turn the tool into a habit. And they turn the habit into better thinking.

Run charts help you see the story over time. They show if something is changing. But they do not tell you if the change is ***noise or signal***. That is where most leaders slip. They see a spike and assume a fix is needed. Or they see a drop and think something broke. That is not always true. Sometimes the system is just doing what systems do: fluctuating. And if you act on every bump, you create more chaos than clarity. That is why the next tool matters.

Control charts go one level deeper. They take the same data, but they frame it with limits that tell you what normal actually looks like. Not what you hope. What the process can reliably deliver. Control charts are not complicated. But they are powerful. They keep leaders from overreacting. They show when to act and when to leave it alone. Let's walk through how to use them the right way. With purpose. With clarity. And without getting lost in the noise.

Control Chart

What It Tells You

A control chart tells you if a process is stable or unstable. That is it. Not if the number is good. Not if the goal was hit. Just whether the process is behaving the way it usually does. That distinction matters. Because you can miss a target and still have a stable process. You can hit a target and still have a process that is falling apart underneath. A control chart strips away the emotion and gives you a simple answer: is this variation normal or is something in the system shifting.

It does that by plotting your data points over time and adding control limits. These limits are calculated based on how the process has behaved before. If the data stays inside those limits and does not show certain patterns, the process is considered in control. That does not mean it is where you want it. It means it is consistent. It means the variation you are seeing is coming from the system itself. Not a special cause. Not a one time issue. It is how the system runs.

This chart helps leaders make better decisions. Instead of reacting to every data point, you can step back and ask a better question: is the process stable. If it is, you improve the process. If it is not, you look for what changed. That simple split is what makes the tool powerful. It turns noise into signal and guessing into action.

When to Use It

Use a control chart when you need to know if the variation in your results is something to worry about or just part of how the process works. That means using it when people start asking, what happened here. Use it when teams are feeling whiplash from targets moving in and out of range and no one knows if the system is the problem or just the day.

Control charts are especially helpful in steady operations where the work is repeatable. Think approvals per day, customer response time, defects per batch. If you are tracking something over time and the conversation keeps jumping from one data point to the next, this chart helps bring the team back to the bigger picture.

They are also useful when the organization is in improvement mode. If you are testing changes and want to know if they are actually making a difference, control charts give you a grounded answer. Not just, the number moved. But, the system changed. That is the proof that makes improvement real.

Use them when people start blaming the process for what is really random noise. Use them when leadership is overreacting to every data point. Use them when the conversation needs to shift from results to system behavior. That is what control charts are for.

What to Watch For

First, look for any point outside the control limits. That is a clear signal something changed. It is not just a high or low number. It is statistically unlikely to happen unless the process was altered. That could be a shift in volume, a new way of working, or a breakdown somewhere upstream. Do not jump to fix the outcome. Find what changed in the system.

Next, watch for runs. That means a series of points all above or all below the center line. If the data stays on one side for too long, the process might have shifted. It is not random. It is drifting. That drift might be subtle, but it matters. It is telling you the system is not the same as it was before.

Also watch for trends. If the data is consistently moving in one direction, up or down, that is not noise. It might still be within limits, but it is a sign something is changing. Ask what has been adjusted. Ask what got added or removed. Ask if people are stretching to make the number or if the number is changing on its own.

Finally, pay attention to how tightly the data clusters. If the points are suddenly more spread out than they used to be, the process might be unstable even if the average has not changed. Wide variation means the team is probably struggling behind the scenes to keep things on track.

You will know the chart is helping when the conversation stops jumping from point to point and starts asking about the system. You will know it is helping when leaders stop overreacting and start listening. You will know it is helping when the team can explain what normal looks like and what it does not.

> A control chart does not fix anything. But it keeps you from fixing the wrong thing. It gives you a way to lead with calm, clear thinking when everyone else wants to panic. That is what makes it worth using. Not the math. The mindset. The discipline to wait until the system tells you it is time to act.

Control charts help you see when the system itself is changing. They show if the variation you are seeing is expected or if something underneath has shifted. That is what makes them powerful. But once you know the system is off, you still have to figure out why. You still have to get to the root of what is causing the change. That is where the next tool comes in. It does not look at results. It looks at causes. It helps you and the team organize the thinking so the real issue does not get buried under guesses or noise. Let's walk into the next tool. One that brings clarity when everything feels tangled. Let's talk about the cause and effect diagram.

Scatter Plot

What It Tells You

A scatter plot shows the relationship between two things. One goes on the horizontal axis. The other goes on the vertical. Each point is a moment in time where both things happened together. You step back and look for a pattern. Are they moving together? Are they moving in opposite directions? Or is there no pattern at all?

This tool does not prove anything. It does not say one thing caused another. What it does is give you a picture of the relationship. It shows if two variables are linked closely enough that it is worth asking more. That is the job. Not to confirm what you already believe. To test if the connection is even there.

A scatter plot is useful because most arguments about what causes what are based on opinion. People say, "When this goes up, that goes down." A scatter plot says, "Let's see." It clears the fog. If the pattern is there, you can move forward with confidence. If it is not, you stop chasing shadows.

When to Use It

Use a scatter plot when you have two metrics and you want to test if they are moving together. Not just once. Consistently. This is helpful when someone says, "We think X is affecting Y." The scatter plot answers, "Show me." It is also helpful when you are seeing variation and want to know what might be driving it. Cycle time and volume. Defects and time of day. Errors and experience level. This tool gives you a way to look for that link.

Use it after you build a cause and effect diagram and want to test which causes are real. Or after an improvement and you want to confirm whether the change actually influenced the outcome. You are not proving cause. You are looking for correlation. That is enough to make better decisions.

This is not a tool for day one of problem solving. It comes in after the thinking starts. It helps you move from conversation to confirmation. It is not for tracking. It is for testing.

What to Watch For

Watch for the shape. If the points rise together in a line, that is a positive correlation. If one rises while the other falls, that is negative. If the points are scattered with no shape, there is no correlation. That does not mean the idea was wrong. It means the data does not back it up. That is useful too. It keeps you from fixing what was not broken.

Also watch for outliers. One or two points far from the rest can throw off your thinking. They might need a closer look. But they should not define the story. The goal is to see the pattern, not chase the exception.

Ask yourself three questions. Does the pattern make sense? Is it strong enough to act on? And does it change how we see the problem? If the answer is yes, move forward. If not, ask what else might be influencing the result. Use the chart to guide your next round of learning.

You will know this tool is working when the conversation moves from "we think" to "we see." When the team starts checking their assumptions before jumping into a fix. When the next step is based on what is visible, not what is loud.

Scatter plots do not solve the problem. They shine a light on what matters. And once you see the link, the next step is figuring out how big the problem really is. That is where the next tool comes in. It helps you see the spread. The variation. The range of performance when things go right and when they go wrong. It is not about the average. It is about what surrounds it. Let's look at the histogram.

Histogram

What It Tells You

A histogram shows how something is distributed. Not the total. Not the average. The spread. It tells you how often different values show up and whether that pattern makes sense. You see if the process is consistent or scattered. You see if results are tightly grouped or all over the map. That shape matters. Because it shows you what normal looks like and what sits outside of it.

This tool is not about tracking a single result. It is about stepping back to see how the system behaves across time. It shows if most outcomes are predictable or if there is too much variation to trust what will happen next. The histogram does not give you the reason. But it gives you the shape of the problem. And that is where good problem solving begins.

When to Use It

Use a histogram when you are looking at a process that runs often and gives you a lot of data. Think cycle time, handling time, wait time, lead time, or anything with variation that repeats. This tool is useful early in the process when you are trying to understand how a system behaves. It is also helpful after a change when you want to see if results got tighter or just shifted.

Use it when people are debating how bad the problem is. When averages are hiding extremes. When the range of performance matters more than the mean. If a report says the average turnaround time is three days, but half the cases take one and the other half take five, you do not have a three-day problem. You have a spread problem. A histogram shows that clearly.

This is also the tool to use when you are testing if your improvement actually reduced variation. If the shape gets narrower, that means more consistency. That matters. Because consistency builds trust. Not just in performance. In process.

What to Watch For

Look at the shape. If the bars form a tight curve in the center, that is a good sign. The process is predictable. If they spread wide or have multiple peaks, you have work to do. Multiple peaks often mean different processes are being mixed together. Different teams. Different inputs. Different standards. The histogram is not just showing noise. It is showing that the process is not one process. That is a root cause in disguise.

Also look for long tails. If most results are clustered but a few stretch way out, those outliers need attention. Not because they are bad. Because they might be showing you something the average hides. They could be exceptions. They could be early signs of something breaking down.

Ask these questions. Is the range of outcomes acceptable? Do the peaks make sense based on how the process runs? Is there more than one story hidden in the same data? That last one is key. Histograms often show you when you are treating one problem like it is the same for everyone. It is not.

You will know the histogram is working when the conversation shifts from "what's the average" to "what is really happening." When leaders stop chasing single numbers and start asking how tight the system runs. When improvement means more consistency, not just better performance.

The histogram helps you see the shape of the system. It shows you how results are spread, where the variation lives, and what might be hiding behind averages. But once you understand the distribution, you still need to track how often those issues show up and where. You need a way to collect that truth from the front line, without filters or delay. That is where the next tool comes in. It is not a graph. It is not a report. It is a habit. A simple way to gather data at the source and make the invisible real. Let's talk about the check sheet.

Check Sheet

What It Tells You

A check sheet shows you what is really happening in the work. Not what people remember. Not what gets reported up. What actually occurs. It tracks how often something happens and when. Nothing fancy. Just a simple way to collect facts in real time at the source. That is what makes it powerful. Because most systems do not fail from lack of data. They fail from lack of truth.

The check sheet gives you that truth. It makes patterns visible before they get buried in a summary. It does not analyze. It captures. It shows where problems live, how often they show up, and whether they are getting better or worse. This is not about documentation. This is about focus. You cannot fix what you do not see. The check sheet helps you see it.

When to Use It

Use a check sheet when you need real-time data to understand where the pain is coming from. It is especially useful early in problem solving when the team says, "we think it's a problem" but no one can prove it. You use a check sheet to track frequency. To get out of the anecdote and into the pattern.

This tool is helpful when you are hearing noise but do not know where to start. Are errors happening more on one shift than another? Are delays showing up at a certain step? Are certain types of issues driving most of the rework? The check sheet helps answer those questions without guessing.

It is also the right tool when you are trying to measure the impact of a change. If you adjusted a process, and you want to see if the issue went down, the check sheet tracks that. Day by day. One mark at a time. No wait. No filter. Just facts.

What to Watch For

Look for patterns in what is being marked. What is showing up most? What time of day does it happen? Is one category dominating the sheet? These answers matter because they guide where to look next. The goal is not just to collect data. The goal is to find the story it tells.

Watch how the sheet is being used. If marks are missing or everything is listed as "other," the format needs work. Make it easier. Fewer categories. Clearer definitions. Track only what you need. If people are not using it, the design is too complex or the point is unclear.

Also pay attention to how the team talks about the check sheet. If they see it as a task, it becomes noise. If they see it as a way to improve the process, it becomes useful. That is the shift you are looking for. The tool is only as good as the trust behind it.

You will know the check sheet is working when the team starts saying, "we've seen this five times this week" and they are right. When the data is coming from the work, not the memory. When the focus is sharper and the next step is clearer.

The check sheet does not fix the issue. It shows you where to start. It turns opinions into facts. It gives the team a way to track what matters and the leader a way to act on what is real. Used well, it builds discipline without complexity. And it earns trust. One mark at a time.

In Summary

These tools are not complicated. But they are powerful. When used the right way, they help you lead with clarity. Not by guessing. By seeing. By asking better questions. By taking smarter action. The tools help. But they are not the answer. They are the support. The structure. The part that keeps the thinking honest. But knowing how to use the tools is only part of it. Knowing what to look for matters just as much. Waste hides in plain sight. It drains time, energy, and trust. If you cannot see it, you cannot solve it. The next chapter breaks that down. The eight wastes. What they look like. Why they matter. And how leaders can start making them visible. Let's get into it.

Chapter Eleven

The Eight Wastes of Lean for Leaders

Most waste does not show up in a report. It shows up in how the work feels. Tasks get repeated. People wait. Information gets chased. Quality slips. Time gets filled without results. The numbers might not blink, but the team feels it every day. The last chapter gave you tools to see the problem. This one helps you see what is causing it. Not in theory. In real time. Waste is not a Lean word. It is what gets in the way of doing good work.

Every system has it. No team is immune. What separates strong leadership is not whether waste exists; it is whether you can spot it, name it, and do something useful in response. This chapter is not about learning new terms. It is about sharpening your eyes. Each of the eight wastes shows up in different ways, but they all share one thing: they hide in plain sight. You will not find them unless you are looking. And once you see them, the right questions matter more than the right answer.

We are going to walk through each waste from a leadership angle. Not to define it. To recognize it. To understand what it sounds like, where it hides, what causes it, and what to do about it. Not as a one time fix. As a discipline. That is what Lean leadership really is. Not knowing the tools. Seeing the drift. Asking the right questions. Supporting the team. And removing what does not belong.

Let's start with the most common one. The one that feels like work but adds nothing. Let's start with overproduction.

Overproduction

What It Looks Like

Overproduction in a transactional setting is not about printing too many reports or making too many copies. It is when work is done before it is needed, faster than it is needed, or in greater volume than what is actually required. It shows up as teams pushing tasks downstream before the next person is ready. It shows up as reports that no one uses, emails that cover too much too early, or systems that automatically generate work that no one asked for yet. It creates pileups. It overwhelms the next step. And it hides behind the illusion of productivity. The team looks busy. But they are working ahead of need. That is not helpful. That is waste.

How to Spot It

Look for backlogs where no one is asking for more. Look for queues that grow even when the demand is stable. Listen for phrases like "we always prep it just in case" or "we send it early so we're not the delay." Those are signs. Watch for steps that are repeated later because they were done too soon and had to be redone. The clearest signal is rework that comes from working ahead of clarity. If the team keeps touching the same task more than once, they are not being proactive. They are overproducing.

What Causes It

Most overproduction comes from fear. Fear of being blamed for a delay. Fear of not being ready. Fear of idle time being mistaken for slacking. Leaders push teams to stay busy, so people produce even when the system is not ready to receive. Automation makes it worse. A rule gets built into a system, and suddenly it triggers work around the clock whether it is needed or not. Volume goes up. Value does not.

What to Do About It

Slow the system down. Ask what the customer actually needs and when they need it. Then pull the work based on that need. Do not let upstream teams push based on capacity.

Let downstream need set the pace. Review reports and outputs regularly. Ask who uses them. If no one raises a hand, stop making them. Make it okay to have capacity without filling it. Make it normal to wait for the right time instead of defaulting to early action. Overproduction looks like urgency. But it is just noise. You do not fix it by working harder. You fix it by staying aligned to what is needed now. Not what might be needed later.

Waiting

What It Looks Like

Waiting is the quietest waste. It does not make noise. It does not leave a mess. But it slows everything down. In transactional work, waiting shows up when tasks sit in queues, approvals take days, or systems leave people stuck without what they need to move forward. It is the handoff that sits in an inbox. It is the form that needs a signature but no one knows who owns it. It is the ticket that just says pending. The team is ready. The work is not. That is waste.

How to Spot It

Look at cycle time versus touch time. If a task takes ten minutes to complete but five days to get through the process, you are staring at a waiting problem. Ask how long things sit before someone touches them. Ask how many steps require someone else to act before the team can move. Track how often people say, "I'm waiting on..." If that phrase is part of the daily vocabulary, you have a system issue. Waiting also shows up when teams batch their work because they know the next step is slow. They do not want to send it over one at a time. That is a signal. The process is broken.

What Causes It

Waiting is often baked into the way the system was designed. Roles are separated. Tools are disconnected. Approvals are layered. Everyone touches the work, but no one owns the flow. Sometimes it is caused by fear. People hold onto work longer than needed to avoid scrutiny. Sometimes it is policy. A rule says wait for a full batch or a full day or a full review before moving. Sometimes it is just habit. That is the way we've always done it. The problem is that while the work waits, the customer does too. And that cost is real.

What to Do About It

Map the flow. Find the dead zones. Name them. Waiting hides in between the steps, so make those gaps visible. Ask what would happen if the step was skipped or the handoff was faster. Push decisions closer to the work. Remove approvals that do not add value. Automate where it makes sense, but only if it removes delay, not just effort. And do not reward the team for clearing the backlog if no one asks why it built up in the first place. Speed does not fix waiting. Only flow does. Make the flow real. Make the blockers visible. Then remove them one at a time. Waiting is not part of the job. It is the space where progress used to be.

Rework

What It Looks Like

Rework is the cost of getting it wrong the first time. It is not always dramatic. Sometimes it hides. A form gets sent back. A ticket gets reopened. A customer calls again to clarify something they already explained. Rework in transactional work is anything that has to be done twice when once should have been enough. It is the second follow-up. The missed detail. The correction that feels normal but is actually waste. Every time something loops back instead of moving forward, that is rework.

How to Spot It

Ask how often things come back. How often does a task leave the team and return because something was missed. Look at error rates. Look at reopened cases. Look at the time spent fixing what was already done. Rework is also in the shadow work, the emails clarifying what a request meant, the meetings that should have been avoided if the input was clearer. It is everywhere, but it feels normal. That is what makes it dangerous. Most teams expect it. They build time around it. But it is still waste.

What Causes It

Rework is usually caused by unclear inputs, broken handoffs, or inconsistent standards. Someone upstream was not sure what was needed. Someone downstream made an assumption. The process relies too much on memory or individual style. It is often made worse by pressure. Teams rush, miss something, and have to fix it later. Leaders say "just get it done," and the rework gets baked into the routine. When teams are solving the same problems every week, the cause is not people. It is the process.

What to Do About It

Do not punish rework. Study it. Track where it shows up. Ask what went wrong, not who. Go back to the handoff. Go back to the instructions. Go back to the system that let the mistake happen without catching it. Standardize the inputs. Make expectations clear. Teach teams to stop when something feels off instead of fixing it after the fact. Give them space to slow down where it matters so they do not have to repeat the work later. Rework is not fixed by going faster. It is fixed by going better.

Overprocessing

What It Looks Like

Overprocessing is doing more than what is needed to get the job done. In transactional environments, it shows up as extra steps, extra checks, extra formatting, and extra touches that do not change the outcome. A report with ten tabs when three will do. A deck built for one update that could have been an email. A process with three levels of approval because someone once made a mistake. These things look helpful. But if they do not add value for the customer or the team, they are waste.

THE EIGHT WASTES OF LEAN FOR LEADERS

How to Spot It

Look at how much effort goes into getting the final result. Ask if every step adds something real. If the team is copying data from one system to another, formatting for optics, or creating documentation no one uses, that is overprocessing. If work is being checked multiple times without errors being caught, that is overprocessing. If there are templates for templates or reports that no one reads, that is the signal. Not everything that looks polished is useful. Not everything that is compliant is helpful.

What Causes It

Most overprocessing starts with good intent. A team wants to be thorough. A leader wants to avoid mistakes. A past issue created pressure, so a new check was added and never removed. Over time, these layers grow. And because they are familiar, no one questions them. The fear of being wrong outweighs the cost of doing too much. That is how the system gets heavy. Not from failure. From protection.

What to Do About It

Audit the process from the customer's point of view. Ask what they actually care about. Ask what step would be missed if it disappeared. Review documentation and output. Ask what gets used. Ask what gets ignored. Make it safe to remove what no longer serves the work. Lead with the mindset that clear beats clever and useful beats polished. If something is being done "just in case," challenge it. Overprocessing feels safe. But it drains time and hides the real issues. Removing it is not risky. It is respectful.

Inventory

What It Looks Like

Inventory in transactional work is not about shelves or stockrooms. It is work sitting in queues. It is emails waiting in inboxes. It is approvals stuck in the system. It is backlog.

Open cases. Unread tickets. Anything that has started but not finished. You cannot see it on a shelf, but it is there. And it is holding up value. The more inventory you have, the more time gets lost to rechecking, restarting, and reprioritizing. The system might look busy. But the customer is still waiting.

How to Spot It

Look at the gaps between start and finish. Look at the stack of open items. Look at the volume of in-progress work that no one is working on. That is inventory. Look at the number of handoffs. The number of teams involved. Every time the work stops moving and waits for the next person, it is inventory. Ask how long the average ticket or case sits before someone acts. Not how long it takes to finish. How long it sits. That is the waste.

What Causes It

Most inventory builds up because the system allows it. Too many priorities. No work in process limits. Approval layers. Capacity mismatches. Leaders asking for everything at once. Teams trying to do too much at once. All of that creates a pileup. No one wants to be the reason something is delayed, so everything gets started. But not everything gets finished. That is how the system clogs. Not from inaction. From too much in motion.

What to Do About It

Limit what gets worked on at once. Make work in progress visible. Use Kanban or a visual board. Keep the team focused on flow, not volume. Prioritize finishing over starting. Stop measuring how much is assigned. Start measuring how much is moving. Ask how long work sits. Then ask what is keeping it there. Work with upstream and downstream partners to balance the flow. You do not need more hands. You need better pacing. The goal is not to clear the backlog. The goal is to prevent it from building up again.

Motion

What It Looks Like

Motion in transactional work is every extra step that does not move the outcome forward. It is jumping between systems to find the right data. It is digging through folders to locate a form. It is scrolling through emails to piece together what happened. It is toggling. Searching. Repeating. The work might be moving, but the value is not. That is motion. And it shows up in quiet ways that wear people out without ever showing up on a report.

How to Spot It

Watch the steps it takes to complete a task. Not the big milestones. The in-between. How many systems does the person touch? How many windows are open? How often do they stop to check with someone else? How often do they have to retype, relog, or rework just to keep moving? That is not just part of the job. That is waste. You will also see it in the questions people ask: Where do I find that? Who owns this? Which version is right? Each of those is a signal. Too much motion. Not enough clarity.

What Causes It

Motion waste comes from broken processes pretending to be normal. Legacy systems that do not talk to each other. Documentation stored in twenty places. Workflows built by workarounds. No one designed it this way. It just happened. And because no one owns it, it stays broken. The more disconnected the tools, the more motion it takes to hold the system together. And that motion becomes part of the job. Until someone calls it out.

What to Do About It

Map the process at the task level. Not just who hands what to who, but what they actually do. Watch them work. Ask where they go to get information. Count the clicks. Track the toggles. Then ask what can be eliminated, automated, or clarified. Clean up the instructions. Combine systems where you can. Build shared access to data that people keep asking for. Stop making the person compensate for a broken system. Reduce the steps. Shorten the path. Make the process do the work so the people can focus on what matters. Motion adds up. But it is fixable. Once you see it.

Unused Talent

What It Looks Like

This waste shows up in the quiet. In meetings where only the top voices speak. In workflows where smart people do the job but are never asked how to improve it. You will see people following instructions exactly but never offering ideas. You will hear updates but not questions. You will see experienced team members sitting out of the thinking because the system does not ask them to think. The work gets done. But the insight is left on the table.

How to Spot It

Look for meetings that only go one way. Look for updates that never lead to discussion. Look for ideas that stay buried until someone leaves. If the same handful of people are solving every problem, the rest of the talent is being wasted. If new hires learn quickly that decisions live two levels up, they stop sharing what they see. This is not resistance. It is adaptation. You will also notice a pattern in your problems. The same ones come back because the people closest to them were never part of the solution.

What Causes It

The most common cause is structure. Leaders unintentionally create environments where contribution is not expected or rewarded. Roles get rigid. Approval paths get long. Risk is avoided. So people do not try. Sometimes it is history. Teams that lived through failed programs or ignored suggestions learn that silence is safer. Sometimes it is fear. Not of speaking, but of being held responsible if it does not go well. And often it is a culture of speed. We move so fast we forget to ask who knows best. Spoiler alert: it is usually the person doing the work.

What to Do About It

Start asking better questions. Ask what feels harder than it should. Ask what they would fix if they could. Then shut up and listen. Do not ask for ideas unless you are willing to back one. Prove that feedback leads to action. Recognize small wins. Protect experiments. If someone shares a possible fix, clear the space to try it. That act does more for culture than any program. Over time, the questions become normal. And the silence gets replaced with ownership. Not because people were told. Because they were invited.

Excessive Handoffs

What It Looks Like

This waste shows up when the same piece of work passes through too many hands before it gets done. It is a file that gets emailed back and forth five times for one comment. It is a ticket that moves between three queues before anyone takes action. It is when no one owns the whole and everyone owns a slice. The outcome is slow, confusing, and full of rework. And no one feels responsible for how long it took.

How to Spot It

Watch how many people touch a task from start to finish. Count how many times a customer gets transferred. Map the number of approvals needed before something moves. If people spend more time routing or clarifying than actually doing, that is a sign. You will also hear phrases like "I just hand it off" or "not my lane" when something is stuck. That is not process. That is friction. And it costs more than time. It kills *ownership*.

What Causes It

Most of the time it starts with good intent. Segmentation was meant to bring clarity. Handoffs were meant to reduce risk. Roles were created to protect boundaries. But over time, layers stack. The flow breaks. And no one sees the whole picture. Sometimes it is policy. Sometimes it is legacy structure. And sometimes it is habit. People are so used to passing the work along that they stop asking if it could just be done.

What to Do About It

Start by mapping the journey of a single task. Who touches it? Why? What value does each step add? Ask the team where the delays happen. Ask where the decisions are. Then test what can be removed. Combine roles if possible. Eliminate approvals that are never challenged. Give one person ownership of the outcome instead of splitting it across five checkpoints. This is not about speed. It is about flow. And when flow improves, accountability does too. Fix the handoffs and the rest of the system breathes easier.

In Summary

Waste is not always visible. It hides in habits, assumptions, and the way we have always done things. This chapter broke it down so leaders can see it for what it is: unnecessary effort, delay, or complexity that gets in the way of value. You now know what it looks like. You know how to spot it. You know where it comes from and what to do when you see it. But tools and tactics are not enough. Waste comes back if the culture allows it.

The real test of Lean is not what is on the board. It is what happens in the conversations, the coaching, and the way leaders show up when things go sideways. The next chapter is about that. The human side. The part of Lean that cannot be laminated. The part that decides if any of this sticks. Let's talk about the people. Because that is where Lean lives or dies.

Chapter Twelve

The Human Side of Lean

Most Lean efforts do not fail because of the tools. They fail because of how people feel while using them. You can roll out boards, training, and metrics, but if people do not feel safe bringing up problems or trusted to fix them, nothing sticks. The tools might show up, but the behavior will not follow. That is the real barrier. Not knowledge. Not skill. Fear.

The human side of Lean is not about being soft. It is about being honest. People do not resist change because they are lazy. They resist because they have seen it done badly. They have been through programs that promised empowerment but delivered more control. They have raised problems and watched nothing happen. They have spoken up and been shut down. That history stays with them. And if leaders ignore that, they lose the chance to build something better.

This chapter is not about engagement surveys or motivation theories. It is about how leaders build trust through action. It is about creating a culture where speaking up is expected, solving problems is normal, and trying something new is not a risk. This is not extra work. This is the work. If the people doing the work do not believe in the system, the system will fail. The human side is not separate from Lean. It is what makes it real. Let's walk through what that looks like when it is done with purpose.

Psychological Safety is not a Buzzword

Psychological safety is not about being nice. It is about people knowing they can speak up without paying for it. They can call out a broken process, share a mistake, or suggest a better way without fear of getting blamed or ignored. If that safety is not there, they will hold back. And when they hold back, the problems stay hidden. Lean depends on visibility. You cannot improve what no one is willing to say out loud. If people do not feel safe, they stop pointing to the real issues. They nod. They stay quiet. They wait to be told what to do. That is not culture. That is survival. And it will kill every tool you try to use.

You build safety by how you show up when it matters. When someone brings up an issue, do you listen or defend? When a countermeasure fails, do you ask what they learned or what went wrong? When a frontline team member points out something leadership missed, do you thank them or change the subject? These are not soft skills. They are leadership moments. And they tell the team exactly what is allowed and what is not.

You will know safety is building when people stop checking your mood before they speak. When they bring up problems in front of others without being prompted. When they say what is not working without dressing it up. When trying something new is not a risk. It becomes normal.

> Do not say it is safe. Prove it. Every day. With every reaction. That is what earns trust. And without trust, Lean is just another program. Nothing sticks if people do not believe they are safe to be honest. That is not extra. That is the work.

The Research Behind It

Psychological safety is not a trend. It is one of the most studied and proven drivers of team performance. In a multi-year study across hundreds of teams, Google's Project Aristotle found that psychological safety was the number one predictor of high-performing teams. Not skill. Not experience. Safety. The ability to speak freely without fear of embarrassment or retaliation. That was the difference. Harvard researcher Amy Edmondson first defined the concept as a shared belief that the team is safe for interpersonal risk. In her work, teams that had high psychological safety were more likely to report errors and fix them faster. They learned more, adapted faster, and solved problems before they became visible at the top. The teams that looked perfect on paper were often just quiet. And that silence had a cost. In Lean environments, the risk of silence is even higher. Because Lean is built on surfacing problems, testing changes, and learning from failure. If people hold back, you lose the learning. You get surface-level improvement that looks good in reports but falls apart in practice. This is not about being soft. It is about performance. The data shows that safety leads to speed, accuracy, and resilience. You get problems earlier, solutions faster, and teams that take ownership instead of waiting for permission. That is the kind of performance every leader is trying to build.

You do not need a certificate in organizational behavior to act on this. The research confirms what your team already knows. When they feel safe, they engage. When they do not, they shut down. Your daily actions either reinforce that or remove it. The theory is strong. The results are measurable. And the responsibility sits with the leader. Every time.

Trust Is Built Through Repetition

You do not build trust with a kickoff meeting. You build it by showing up the same way over and over until people stop wondering which version of you they are going to get. That is what trust is. Predictability in behavior. When people know you will follow through. When they know you will protect the work. When they know you will not turn on them when something goes wrong.

Leaders break trust when they react one way in front of the group and another way behind closed doors. When they say the team owns the work but take the first real decision for themselves. When they praise problem solving but only reward results. People notice. And once the gap shows up, the trust drops fast. It takes one moment to shake it. It takes a lot longer to earn it back. Trust is not built in big moments. It is built in the boring ones. Showing up on time. Asking the same question every week. Following through when no one reminds you. Doing what you said, even when it is no longer convenient. These are not extras. These are the signals that tell the team if they can count on you or not. You do not need to be perfect. But you need to be consistent. Teams will forgive a mistake. They will not forgive being surprised. Especially not twice.

You will know trust is building when people start speaking up without looking around the room first. When they stop sugarcoating problems. When they tell you the truth even when the result is not good. That does not happen because they believe in Lean. It happens because they believe in you.

If you want people to take ownership, you have to give them a reason to believe they will not be left hanging when they do. Trust is not a trait. It is a pattern. One small action repeated until it becomes the expectation. That is how it grows. And that is how it holds.

The Research Behind It

Trust is not abstract. It shows up in performance. It shows up in retention. It shows up in how fast a team can move without being managed. Multiple studies have proven that trust is one of the strongest drivers of team success. When it is there, people act. When it is not, they hold back. Stephen Covey called trust a force multiplier. His research showed that when trust is low, speed goes down and cost goes up. People pause. They double check. They spend energy protecting themselves. When trust is high, people share more, act faster, and get more done with less friction. Trust makes systems efficient. The absence of trust adds waste you cannot see on a chart. Paul Zak studied the connection between trust and team chemistry. He found that teams with high trust showed more initiative, had stronger problem solving, and produced better results. It did not come from motivational speeches. It came from repeatable actions. Leaders who followed through. Leaders who stayed consistent. Leaders who did what they said, especially when things got hard. In a Lean system, trust is not a nice to have. It is what allows problems to surface without fear. It is what gives people permission to test, learn, and speak up. Without trust, the process breaks down. Not because the tools are wrong. Because the team does not believe they will be backed if something goes wrong.

The data matches what experience already tells us. If people trust you, they tell you the truth. If they do not, they give you silence. You cannot lead a Lean culture through silence. You lead it by showing up the same way every time, until the team knows they can count on it. That is what earns trust. That is what holds it. That is what makes it real.

Respect Means Giving People Control

> Respect is not how you talk. It is how much control you give people over their work. If you say you respect the team but make all the decisions, override their ideas, or step in at the first sign of trouble, the message is clear. You do not trust them. And they will stop trying to lead.

Lean talks a lot about respect for people, but that phrase gets watered down. It turns into politeness or saying thank you. Real respect shows up when leaders stop holding all the control. When they let the team own the process and the problems that come with it. That is not letting go. That is leading the right way. You show respect by asking instead of telling. By staying curious. By waiting just long enough for the team to work it through on their own. You do not need to solve it. You need to make sure the space is there for them to solve it. That is how you develop people. That is how you create ownership. When people have control, they lean in. They start improving the work instead of working around it. They raise problems because they know they can do something about them. That is how the system gets better. Not because you fixed it. Because they did.

You will know you are giving the right level of control when the team makes decisions before you arrive. When they walk you through the fix instead of waiting for approval. When they hold the standard without needing to be reminded. That does not come from training. That comes from trust. And that trust comes from respect that shows up in your behavior, not just your tone.

Control is not something leaders should protect. It is something they should share. The more ownership the team has, the more likely Lean becomes a habit instead of a project. Respect is not what you say. It is what you give. Give control. Give space. Give credit. That is what builds the kind of team that leads itself. And that is what Lean needs to work.

The Research Behind It

Respect in Lean is directly tied to engagement, ownership, and long term performance. Studies show that when people have control over their work, they care more, they solve more, and they stay longer. When they do not, they check out. Even if they stay on the payroll, they are not in the work. Self Determination Theory, one of the most studied models in psychology, says that autonomy is a core human need. Not a perk. A need. People want to feel like they have a say in what they do and how they do it. When that need is met, motivation rises. When it is blocked, people disengage. The Gallup organization found that employees who feel their opinions count are more productive, have fewer safety incidents, and deliver higher customer satisfaction. But the key is not being asked. The key is seeing their input change something. That is what builds respect. Action, not acknowledgement. Toyota's own internal research showed the same thing. Respect for people was not about being agreeable. It was about creating systems where employees could control and improve their work. Supervisors who allowed frontline teams to solve problems saw better results, less turnover, and stronger improvement over time. The ones who held control stalled out.

The theory matches the reality. When leaders give control, teams take ownership. When they hold it back, teams wait. If you want Lean to work, the people doing the work need to believe it belongs to them. That belief does not come from what you say. It comes from how much control you are willing to give. That is what turns respect from a value into a behavior. And that is what makes it matter.

What You Tolerate Becomes the Culture

Culture is not what you put on a slide. It is what you allow to happen without saying something. When a broken process goes unaddressed, that becomes the new standard. When blame slides by, it becomes acceptable. When silence gets rewarded, speaking up feels like a risk. You do not need to announce your culture. You are building it every time you choose what to ignore and what to act on.

Most leaders do not set culture through decisions. They set it through tolerances. The behavior that goes unchecked. The meetings that run long. The problems that stay hidden. The side comments that cut the team. These things add up. Slowly. Quietly. Until they become what people expect. And when people expect dysfunction, they stop trying to change it. This is where leaders carry more weight than they realize. If you say problem solving matters but let teams bury issues, the team learns. If you say we fix what is broken but let bad behavior go because someone is high performing, the team learns. And what they learn is that results matter more than respect. That breaks everything Lean is built on. If you want a strong culture, you need a strong filter. That means calling out the first signs of decay. That means addressing the thing that is small now but will become the norm later. That means holding the line, even when it is uncomfortable.

You will know this is working when the team starts to self correct. When someone says, that is not how we do things here. When the standard is not just something you check, it is something they *protect*. That shift only happens when leaders are consistent with what they walk past and what they stand up to.

> Culture is not a rollout. It is a pattern. And that pattern is set by what you allow to stay in place when no one is watching. If you want better behavior, better thinking, and better results, do not start with what you teach. Start with what you tolerate. That is what defines you. That is what defines the team. That is what becomes the culture.

The Research Behind It

Culture is shaped by behavior. Not by mission statements. Not by values posters. Just what people see and what leaders allow. Edgar Schein, who spent decades studying how culture forms in organizations, made it simple. What leaders pay attention to gets reinforced. What they ignore gets repeated. Over time, those patterns become the culture. A study in *Harvard Business Review* showed that when toxic behavior is tolerated, even from top performers, it spreads. It drags down morale. It increases stress. It pushes good people out. But when leaders call it out early and handle it directly, performance improves. People feel safer. The team gets stronger. The difference was not in the policy. It was in the response. More recent work from *MIT's Sloan Management Review* found that toxic culture was the single biggest reason people quit. Not pay. Not workload. Culture. And the most common cause was not bad people. It was the absence of action. Leaders knew something was wrong but stayed quiet. That silence gave permission. And once permission is given, the damage takes hold fast. In Lean systems, the damage shows up in silence. Problems stay hidden. Standards fade. People stop taking ownership. Not because they do not care. Because they do not see anyone protecting what matters. The tools might still be there, but the culture is gone.

The research is clear. Culture does not form by intention. It forms by repetition. And the leader decides what gets repeated. If you let something slide, the team learns to slide with it. If you hold the line, they learn to hold it too. That is not theory. That is what builds a culture people believe in. Or breaks it. One choice at a time. Every day.

Coaching Without Control

You do not build problem solvers by giving them answers. You build them by asking the right questions and staying out of the way long enough for them to think. Coaching is not about control. It is about discipline. The discipline to slow down, ask, listen, and let people work through the problem without stepping in every time it gets uncomfortable.

Most leaders say they want teams to take ownership. But then they rush in with the fix. They fill in the gaps. They explain what they would do. And just like that, they take the work away. The intent is good. The result is not. The team learns to wait. The team learns the answer will come if they hesitate long enough. And the habit of solving dies before it has a chance to grow.

Real coaching shows up in how you respond to problems. Do you ask what they have tried? Do you ask what they think is causing it? Do you ask what they plan to do next? If you are the one doing most of the talking, you are not coaching. You are managing. And you are reinforcing the very thing you say you are trying to change. You do not need a script. You need presence. You need the discipline to hold the space without filling it. You need to let people think out loud, struggle with the cause, and choose a countermeasure even if it is not perfect. That is how people learn. That is how teams grow. Not by getting it right the first time. By owning the process and learning what works.

You will know it is working when people stop asking for permission and start asking for feedback. When they bring you their thinking, not just their result. When they own the problem and the solution. That does not come from control. It comes from consistent coaching. Quiet. Firm. Supportive. Focused on thinking, not tasks.

You do not scale problem solving by taking over. You scale it by letting go at the right time, for the right reasons, and backing people when they try. That is what real coaching looks like. And that is what builds a culture that can solve without waiting for you to show up.

The Research Behind It

Coaching is not a soft skill. It is a performance driver. The research is clear. Teams that are coached instead of managed build more capability, solve more problems, and sustain change longer. Not because they are more skilled. Because they learn to think for themselves. Edgar Schein wrote that the job of a coach is not to give answers. It is to help people uncover their own. When leaders ask questions instead of offering solutions, it creates ownership. And ownership is what separates temporary improvement from long term change. Studies from the Center for Creative Leadership found that teams with strong coaching support perform better under pressure. They adapt faster. They take more initiative. But only when coaching is consistent. One time is not enough. Coaching becomes effective when it becomes expected. The Lean Enterprise Institute has shown the same results. Organizations that focus on coaching as a core leadership behavior see stronger engagement, faster problem resolution, and deeper learning across teams. But only when leaders resist the urge to take over. When they ask instead of tell. When they let the team struggle just long enough to grow.

This is not a theory about being hands off. It is about being deliberate. Coaching works when leaders are present but do not dominate. When they create the space for learning and protect it with consistency. That is what the data shows. That is what the best teams experience. Coaching without control builds trust, builds confidence, and builds teams that can run without being managed. That is the goal. And the research backs it up. Every time.

Handling Failure the Right Way

Failure is part of improvement. If everything works the first time, you are not really solving problems. You are playing it safe. Teams that improve fast are not the ones with the best plans. They are the ones who learn quickly when something does not work. That learning only happens if leaders respond the right way. Most teams are not afraid to try. They are afraid to fail in front of leadership. If one test goes sideways and the first response is blame, correction, or silence, that team will not try again. It is not about the mistake. It is about the reaction. The reaction tells them whether it is safe to learn or not. You handle failure the right way by staying steady. You ask what was tested. What was expected. What actually happened. What was learned. You do not ask who made the call. You do not ask why they did not get it right. You do not ask why they did not come to you first. You stay focused on the process, not the person. This does not mean you lower the bar. It means you keep the bar in the right place. You expect learning. You expect ownership. You expect the team to reflect and adjust. But you also give them the space to do it without fear. That is what protects the improvement cycle. Not reward. Not recognition. Just leadership that does not flinch when something goes wrong.

You will know it is working when teams talk about what failed without being defensive. When they share bad results before they are asked. When the focus stays on the process and the next test, not the mistake. That is the shift. The work becomes about learning, not proving.

> Handling failure the right way is not about making people comfortable. It is about making improvement possible. If the cost of a test is trust, no one will test again. If the cost is a conversation and a next step, the team will keep moving. That is what matters. That is what lasts.

The Research Behind It

The fastest learning does not happen in perfect systems. It happens in places where failure is allowed, expected, and used to get better. Amy Edmondson's work at Harvard showed that the highest performing teams were not the ones with the fewest mistakes. They were the ones who talked about their mistakes and learned from them. That was the difference. Her studies across healthcare, manufacturing, and tech all showed the same pattern. When people felt they could speak up after something went wrong, the team improved. When they stayed quiet, performance dropped. Errors stacked up. Trust faded. Not because people did not care. Because they did not feel safe to be honest. The Lean Enterprise Institute found the same thing. The best Lean systems test, learn, and adjust often. But that only works when failure is treated like information. When the reaction to a miss is reflection, not blame. Teams that were punished for trying stopped trying. Teams that were supported after a failed test kept moving. It was never about talent. It was about the environment. One study called it the second failure. The one that happens after the mistake. When a leader responds in a way that shuts people down. That is the one that sticks. That is the one that teaches the team to keep their head down next time. That moment decides whether the system keeps improving or starts pretending.

The research backs up what most leaders already know. If your response to failure is sharp, the team will stay quiet. If it is steady, the team will learn. That does not mean lowering the standard. It means keeping the standard and making it safe to test your way there. That is how real improvement holds. Not through pressure. Through trust. And trust gets decided every time something goes wrong.

Recognition hat Reinforces the Right Things

Recognition is not about applause. It is about direction. What you choose to notice tells the team what matters. If you only reward outcomes, people chase results. If you call out effort, ownership, and learning, that becomes the behavior they repeat. Recognition shapes culture one comment at a time. Most teams are not short on wins. They are short on visibility. The right work happens quietly. A fix is made. A delay is removed. A problem gets solved before it spreads. When that work gets ignored, people stop doing it. Not out of spite. Out of focus. Attention drives behavior. And if the only attention goes to metrics or fire drills, that is where the energy will go. You do not need a program to recognize the right things. You need presence. You need to say something when someone improves a process. You need to call it out when a team reflects after something fails. You need to say thank you when someone speaks up with honesty. That is what teaches people what this culture values. Not the slide deck. The moment. Recognition works best when it is specific. Say what was done. Say why it mattered. Say what it helped fix. That makes it real. That makes it stick. Generic praise feels good but does not guide behavior. Clear recognition builds alignment and confidence without creating a spotlight culture.

You will know it is working when teams start repeating the right behaviors without being asked. When people bring forward small wins because they know you care about them. When recognition happens across the team, not just from the top. That is the shift. Improvement becomes normal. Not because it was announced. Because it was noticed.

Recognition is not about morale. It is about reinforcing the culture you want. What you choose to see becomes what people expect to repeat. That is leadership. That is how improvement becomes a habit. Quiet. Focused. Consistent. One real moment at a time.

The Research Behind It

Recognition does more than make people feel seen. It tells them what matters. Research from Gallup shows that employees who receive meaningful recognition are more productive, more engaged, and more likely to stay. But the impact is not in the praise. It is in the clarity. Teams that know what gets noticed adjust their focus to match it. That is what makes recognition powerful. Studies from MIT and the *Harvard Business Review* have shown that recognition tied to learning, teamwork, and problem solving has more impact than recognition tied to performance alone. When people are only rewarded for results, they take fewer risks. They play it safe. But when the reward is tied to how the result was reached, people take initiative. They try new things. They improve the system. Daniel Kahneman's work in behavioral economics supports this. He found that what gets rewarded gets repeated, even in small amounts. A simple acknowledgment of effort, improvement, or thoughtful action is enough to shift behavior. Not because of the praise itself. Because it sends a signal. It shows what the culture values. In Lean systems, that signal matters. If you say continuous improvement is the goal but only reward output, you create confusion. If you say problem solving matters but ignore the people doing it, they stop bringing the effort. Recognition closes that gap. It shows alignment between what you say and what you notice.

The research is clear. Recognition changes behavior. But only when it is specific, timely, and tied to something that supports the bigger system. You do not need more awards. You need more moments. Recognition is not about being nice. It is about reinforcing what works. And doing it often enough that the team starts to carry it without you. That is when it sticks. That is when it spreads. That is when it lasts.

Leader Roadmap: How to Start Recognition That Reinforces the Right Things

Step 1: Decide what to reinforce

Before you say anything, be clear about what matters. Are you trying to build problem solving? Consistency in standard work? More ownership? More learning from failure? Pick one or two core behaviors that matter right now. That becomes your filter. You do not need to praise everything. You need to reinforce the things that build the culture.

Step 2: Make it visible, not formal

Use team huddles, one on ones, or casual hallway conversations. You are not giving out awards. You are showing the team what good looks like. Keep it public, but keep it normal. You are setting a tone, not throwing a party.

Step 3: Be specific

Do not say "good job." Say what the person did. Say why it mattered. Say what changed because of it. Example: "You noticed the delay in the approval step, mapped it, and tested a simple fix. That cleared up two hours of waiting every day. That is what improvement looks like." That sticks. That teaches. That gets repeated.

Step 4: Make it frequent, not forced

Look for one thing every day worth calling out. Write it down if it helps you remember. Say it when the moment comes. This is not about being overly positive. It is about noticing the right things and saying something. The repetition builds the habit. The consistency builds the expectation.

Step 5: Shift recognition to the team

Once the habit starts, ask the team who they think made something better this week. Let them name it. Let them say why it mattered. That spreads ownership. That turns recognition from something the leader gives to something the culture carries.

Step 6: Keep it real

If something is not worth calling out, do not force it. People know the difference between recognition and filler. This is about credibility. The moment you start making it a quota, it loses its value. Speak up when it matters. That is what makes it stick.

You will know this is working when improvement starts getting shared before you ask. When teams bring small wins to the surface. When people start noticing each other's impact. Not to get credit. To stay aligned. That is when recognition stops being a task and starts becoming part of how the work gets done. Quiet. Focused. Reinforcing what matters. Every day. That is leadership. That is Lean. That is how you make it last.

When Leaders Break Trust

Every leader will break trust at some point. You will say the wrong thing. You will react too fast. You will make a promise you cannot keep. That moment does not have to define you, but how you respond to it will. In Lean, trust is everything. When it breaks, even a little, the silence comes back. People stop speaking up. They stop trying. They stop believing. Most trust is not lost in big moments. It is lost in small ones. You interrupt when someone brings up a problem. You skip a go see that was on the calendar. You ask for feedback, then do nothing with it. You meant well. But what people saw was inconsistency. And in Lean, inconsistency breaks everything.

You cannot lead a problem solving culture without trust. You cannot ask people to experiment if they think you will punish the outcome. You cannot ask them to speak honestly if you react poorly when they do. Once the gap opens, the only way to close it is to name it and own it. When you break trust, say so. Do not explain it away. Do not wait for it to fade. Tell the team what you missed. Tell them what you learned. Tell them what you are going to do differently. And then do it. Over and over. Until your actions reset the pattern.

You will know the repair is working when the team starts speaking up again. When the tension drops. When the behavior shifts back. But it will not happen fast. And it will not happen because you said the right thing. It will happen because you did the right thing long enough for people to believe it again.

Breaking trust does not make you a bad leader. Ignoring it does. Owning it and fixing it is how you lead better. Not by being perfect. By being real. That is what teams respect. And that is what gives Lean the foundation it needs to grow. Trust is not a bonus. It is the system. And when it breaks, you fix it. That is the work.

The Research Behind It

Research shows that when trust is broken, performance drops fast and recovery takes time. The Leadership Challenge by Kouzes and Posner found that trust is the single most important factor in whether people will follow a leader through change. Not skill. Not vision. Trust. Once it is lost, it becomes the barrier to every next step. A study from the Journal of Trust Research confirmed that broken trust in the workplace leads to reduced engagement, lower collaboration, and a decline in discretionary effort. But it also found something else. Leaders who acknowledged the breach and made visible behavior changes could rebuild trust over time. The key was consistency. Not apology. Repetition. Harvard Business School professor Frances Frei explains that trust is built on three things: authenticity, logic, and empathy. When one slips, trust breaks. Most of the time, it is not about failure. It is about how the leader responded. If the leader acts defensive or distant, people disconnect. But when the leader admits the mistake and shows a change, people start to reengage. The neuroscience backs it up. Studies from the Center for Neuroeconomics show that trust is more likely to be restored when the brain sees a clear signal that the environment has changed. That signal is behavior. Words do not activate it. Repeated action does.

The research is clear. When trust is broken, the only way back is through behavior. Not a new policy. Not a speech. What you do next decides if the team believes again or keeps protecting themselves. Leaders are human. Mistakes will happen. But Lean only survives in environments where trust is repaired, not ignored. The research proves it. Your team already knows it. The rest is up to how you show up.

Leader Reflection: Where Do You Stand on Trust?

Take ten minutes. No audience. No edits. Just you and the truth. Trust is not built by intention. It is built by behavior. These questions are not for a worksheet. They are for you. Quietly. Honestly. Answer them without filters. Then choose what you are going to do about it.

1. When someone brings up a problem, how do you respond

Do you listen. Do you jump in. Do you start offering solutions before they finish talking. Think back to your last few reactions. What did they learn about you based on what you did.

2. What do people expect from you when something fails

Do they expect support. Do they expect frustration. Do they expect silence. Your reaction sets the tone for everything that comes next. If people wait to see your mood, trust is not there.

3. Do you say you want ownership but still hold the control

Can your team make a decision without checking first. Do they lead the fix or wait for you to guide it. Think about whether your behavior matches what you say you want.

4. Who brings up problems without being asked

When was the last time someone surfaced a real issue on their own. If it has been a while, ask yourself if the issues are really gone or if the team just does not think it is worth the risk to speak up.

5. What do you do when you get it wrong

Do you name it. Do you move on and adjust. Or do you explain it away. Trust is not built when you are right. It is built by how you handle being wrong in front of the team.

> **Now do something with it.** Select one answer that does not sit right. Write down the habit behind it. Then write what you will do differently this week. Do not make it formal. Do not make it public. Just start doing it. And keep doing it. That is how trust gets built. Not through talk. Through action.

In Summary

Lean does not live in tools. It lives in people. If the team does not feel safe, supported, and trusted, nothing sticks. This chapter was not about being softer. It was about being real. You cannot ask for ownership without giving it. You cannot expect problem solving if people are punished for getting it wrong. You cannot build a culture on silence and expect the truth to show up in the metrics. You build a Lean system by building the environment where Lean behavior can happen. That takes trust. That takes presence. That takes consistency. You shape that culture by what you reinforce, what you tolerate, and how you show up when things go sideways. The tools are only as strong as the people using them. And the people are only as strong as the leadership behind them. If the culture is not there, no tool will fix it. If the culture is strong, the tools will take root. That is the human side of Lean. And it is not a separate effort. It is the foundation. Everything else rests on it.

But, building Lean is not the finish line. It is the starting point. The real challenge is keeping it. Not for a quarter. Not for the launch window. For good. Systems fade. Culture slips. Priorities shift. If you are not watching, Lean turns into compliance. This next chapter is about how to stop that from happening. It is how you protect the work, reinforce the behavior, and lead Lean in a way that actually lasts. Let's talk about how to sustain the transformation. For real. For the long haul.

Chapter Thirteen

Sustaining the Lean Transformation

Starting Lean is not the hard part. Keeping it is. Anyone can roll out a board or run a few events. Anyone can launch training or talk about culture. The real test comes after. When the spotlight moves on. When the leader changes. When the daily pressure returns. That is when most Lean efforts start to fade. Not because people stop caring. Because no one is protecting the work. Sustaining Lean is not about the tools. It is about the thinking behind them. It is about the discipline to stay with it after the energy of the launch wears off. If the habits do not hold, the system breaks. If the conversations do not continue, the culture slides back to where it started. That is what makes this hard.

This chapter is not about maturity models or checklists. It is about what leaders do to hold the line. It is about how they build routines that keep Lean alive without needing to restart it every year. It is about how they respond when the pull of old habits shows up. And it will show up.

> Lean is not something you set and forget. It is something you lead. Every day. Quiet. Consistent. With just enough pressure to keep the right things moving. Let's walk through what that looks like in practice. This is not about more work. This is about protecting what you already built. That is what makes it last. That is what makes it real.

Make It a Leadership System, Not a Project

If Lean feels like a project, it will be treated like one. That means it gets attention at the start, energy in the middle, and silence when something new shows up. That is the cycle that kills most transformations. Not because people did not care. Because no one made Lean part of how the work is led. You do not sustain Lean by making it a separate effort. You sustain it by making it the way leaders lead. That means the language changes. That means huddles are not an extra meeting. Visual boards are not reports. Standard work is not paperwork. These are not Lean tools. They are how you manage the work. Every day. Without waiting for a problem or a push.

The shift happens when Lean stops being something you check in on and starts being something you use to guide decisions. You ask what the problem is. You ask what the team has already tried. You ask how they know the change worked. Not because it is a Lean checklist. Because it is what strong leaders ask. That is how the system becomes leadership.

You will know this shift has started when leaders stop asking what they are supposed to do and start asking how to do it better. When they use a board because it helps, not because it was assigned. When the cadence holds without reminders. When reviews focus on learning, not blame. That is the difference. That is the goal.

Lean does not need a champion. It needs leaders who use it. Quietly. Repeatedly. As the default way to see the work and support the people in it. When that happens, Lean is no longer the system you are trying to build. It becomes the system you already have. And that is what makes it last.

The Research Behind It

Lean does not fade because the tools were wrong. It fades because leadership never changed. Research from the Lean Enterprise Institute shows that the number one reason Lean efforts fail is not a lack of training or resources. It is that leaders keep leading the same way while asking everyone else to do something different. John Shook, one of the original Lean voices at Toyota, said it clearly. You cannot implement Lean. You have to become Lean. That means how you make decisions, how you coach, and how you manage the work every day has to reflect the system. If those habits do not change, the results will not hold.

The structure might still be there, but the thinking will not be. Edgar Schein's work on culture says the same thing. Culture is built by what leaders consistently pay attention to. If Lean is something you talk about in a meeting but do not use when making decisions, the team sees the gap. And when there is a gap, the culture slides back to what it was before. Not because the team resisted. Because the system allowed it. McKinsey research backs this up. In companies where Lean was built into how leaders ran the business, not as a program but as the way work got done, results were better and held longer. They were not just improving. They were managing differently. That was the difference.

The pattern is simple. If Lean stays outside leadership behavior, it fades. If it becomes how leaders think and act, it stays. That is not a theory. That is what the best systems have in common. And that is what makes Lean stick. Not once. Every day. Without needing a reminder.

Protect the Habits That Hold the System

Lean does not disappear in a day. It slips in pieces. A huddle gets skipped. A board stops being updated. A go see turns into a hallway check-in. The tools are still there, but the habits behind them are gone. That is how Lean fades. Quietly. Slowly. Until what is left looks like Lean but does not work like it. The habits are what hold the system. Not the events. Not the software. Not the posters. The habits. Daily huddles that keep the team aligned. Standard work that locks in the best known way. Visual boards that show what is real. Coaching that pushes thinking. These are not Lean tools. They are leadership habits. And if they do not hold, the culture does not either. Sustaining Lean means protecting these habits. It means making them visible, expected, and nonnegotiable. Not through pressure. Through consistency. A habit is not something you do when there is time. It is something you make time for because you know what happens when it disappears.

You will know the habits are slipping when conversations move back to opinions. When problems get passed up instead of solved at the source. When the metrics are right but the behavior is off. That is when you step in. Not to add pressure. To reset the rhythm.

Lean lives in behavior. If you want it to last, protect the behavior. The system will follow. The culture will hold. But only if the habits stay strong. That is the work. Every day. Repeated. Quiet. Anchored by leadership that does not drift.

The Research Behind It

What gets repeated becomes the system. It is not the rollout that decides if Lean holds. It is the habits that come after. Research from the Toyota Production System and follow-up studies across global industries show the same pattern. When daily habits disappear, performance slips. When they stay consistent, the system holds. The Lean Enterprise Institute studied long term Lean efforts and found that the most common failure point was not lack of knowledge. It was breakdown in execution. Teams stopped doing what worked. Not all at once. Slowly. A skipped huddle here. A quiet board there. Over time, the signals that kept the system aligned went missing. What followed was rework, frustration, and the need to reboot something that was already working.

James Clear, author of *Atomic Habits*, wrote that systems do not rise to the level of goals. They fall to the level of habits. If the structure is strong but the habits fade, the gains will not last. This is true in teams. It is true in leadership. It is true in every place where people are expected to keep improving over time. This matches what every long standing Lean organization has seen firsthand. The tools are not what make it work. It is the rhythm. The check ins. The routines. The way people show up to the work every day. If you want Lean to last, you protect the habits. If you want the system to slip, you start letting them slide.

The research is clear. Habits are not the result of a good system. They are the reason it works. Protect them, and the culture will hold. Let them go, and everything else goes with them. You do not need more training. You need better repetition. That is what makes Lean stick. And that is what keeps it alive.

Review What Matters, Not Just What Moved

If you only review results, that is all the team will focus on. Output will go up. Problems will go underground. Teams will start chasing numbers instead of improving the system. And the moment pressure shows up, shortcuts take over. That is not a culture problem. That is a leadership pattern.

Sustaining Lean means reviewing what actually matters. That includes what moved, but also how it moved and what got in the way. You do not just ask for the metric. You ask for the thinking behind it. You ask what changed. You ask who solved what. You ask what was learned. These questions keep the system honest. They tell the team that how the result was achieved matters just as much as the result itself. This does not mean adding more review time. It means using the time you already spend to reinforce the right behavior. When a leader only reacts to the number, they miss the story. When they ask about process, action, and thinking, they reinforce the culture. Every review is a moment to set the tone. If you skip that, the team starts managing for optics instead of truth.

You will know this is working when teams show their thinking without being asked. When they bring the next improvement with the result. When problems are surfaced before the dip shows up on a chart. That only happens when leaders review more than movement. They review the path that got them there.

You do not lead Lean by watching results. You lead it by reviewing the work that creates them. Quiet. Focused. Real. That is what keeps the system strong when the numbers are not. And that is what makes Lean last.

The Research Behind It

Teams respond to what leaders pay attention to. If all you review is the result, that is what people will focus on. The number will go up. But the thinking will go down. Harvard research confirmed this. Teams that only report outcomes start managing optics. They give updates leaders want to hear. Not what is really happening. That is how problems stay buried until they are too big to ignore. The Lean Enterprise Institute studied long term systems and found the same pattern. When leaders asked about process, ownership, and what was learned, the gains held. When reviews shifted back to just results, the system slipped. The team learned that process only matters until the metric moves. After that, speed wins. And shortcuts come back.

Amy Edmondson's work on psychological safety showed why this happens. When teams are reviewed for outcomes only, they protect themselves. They say less. They avoid risk. But when leaders ask how the work is done and what barriers showed up, people stay honest. Not because it is easy. Because they know the leader actually wants to understand the system.

The research is clear. Review is not a task. It is a message. If the message is that results matter more than the system, the system will break. If the message is that how you get there matters as much as where you land, the habits will hold.

You do not need more time in reviews. You need better questions. The data proves it. The best teams know it. And your behavior confirms it. Every time you choose what to ask and what to skip. That is what sets the tone. That is what sustains the system. That is the work.

Anchor Lean in the Way You Solve Problems

If Lean only shows up in events, it will disappear between them. If it only lives in improvement teams, it will never reach the front line. If it is only used when things go wrong, it becomes a last resort. That is not how you sustain Lean. You sustain it by making it the way problems get solved. Every day. At every level. By everyone. Problem solving is not a special project. It is the work. When a form is wrong, when a delay keeps showing up, when a customer is unhappy, the team should not wait. They should start. A simple five whys. A quick process check. A test of one change. That kind of response is not natural. It is learned. And leaders teach it by how they show up when problems come forward. You keep Lean alive by making that kind of thinking normal. You ask what is causing it. You ask what has been tried. You ask what was learned. Not to check a box. To push clarity. That becomes the habit. And that habit keeps the system moving when the big programs stall out.

You will know it is working when the team brings you thinking, not noise. When they walk you through what they did before you ask. When they fix small things without making a show out of it. That is not luck. That is discipline. That is a system that is rooted in the way problems get solved.

Lean will never hold if it stays separate from daily work. It becomes real when it becomes how the work gets better. Not during a review. Not after the fact. In the moment. That is how you sustain it. And that is where it belongs.

The Research Behind It

Lean holds when problem solving becomes the default response. That is not theory. That is what the research shows. The Lean Enterprise Institute studied systems that sustained over time and found one pattern across all of them. Leaders and teams used the same problem solving behavior every day. They did not wait for events. They did not wait for a coach. They acted. That behavior made the difference. McKinsey research confirmed this. In organizations where Lean was just a toolkit, results faded within a year. But when structured problem solving was used in daily operations, huddles, one on ones, and frontline work, the results stuck. It was not about the size of the problem. It was about the habit. That habit built the resilience that made Lean last.

Toyota has said the same thing for decades. What kept their system strong was not the tool. It was the mindset. The five whys were not saved for big issues. They were used every day by every person. When the team hit a problem, they stopped, thought, acted, and learned. That rhythm was the system. It still is. Edgar Schein spent years studying learning organizations. He found that culture forms around how people respond to gaps. When the gap leads to questions, learning follows. When the gap leads to blame or silence, people shut down. It is not the problem that matters. It is what happens next.

The research is simple. You do not sustain Lean by solving one big problem well. You sustain it by solving small problems often. You do it through habit. Through repetition. Through consistent response. That is what the best teams do. That is what the data shows. And that is how Lean becomes how you work. Not what you say. What you do. Every time.

Manage Turnover Without Losing the System

This is not about creating binders or checklists. It is about making sure the routines are so clear and so normal that a new person steps in and the system keeps going. Huddles still happen. Boards still get updated. Standard work still holds. The questions stay the same. The behavior stays the same. The work stays focused.

> You will know you have built something sustainable when someone new joins the team and the team teaches them the rhythm. Not because they were told. Because it is just what they do. Lean is no longer dependent on who is in charge. It is how the work runs.

If the system falls apart when one person leaves, the system was not strong enough. Your job is not to hold it all together by force. Your job is to build it so it holds on its own. That is how you lead for the long term. And that is what makes Lean last.

How to Attrition-Proof Your Lean System

You cannot stop people from leaving. But you can stop the system from leaving with them. If Lean only works because one person pushes it, then Lean will leave when they do. The goal is not to keep people forever. The goal is to keep the way they work. That is what this guide is for.

1. Lock in the rhythm before people move

Do not wait for a vacancy to fix the gap. Make sure daily huddles, visual boards, problem solving, and standard work are already habits before a transition happens. These are not extras. They are the system. If they are fragile before someone leaves, they will collapse after.

2. Build team-level ownership of Lean routines

The routines should not belong to the manager. They should belong to the team. The team runs the huddle. The team updates the board. The team tracks the metrics. When these habits are shared, they are less likely to fall apart when someone exits. Make ownership clear and shared.

3. Use simple systems to hold the work

Keep Lean tools visible, accessible, and low tech if needed. Whiteboards over dashboards. Checklists over slide decks. If the routine can only be run by the person who built it, it will not survive turnover. The more people who can run the system, the more durable it becomes.

4. Teach the why, not just the tool

People who understand why a board matters or why huddles work will rebuild them when needed. People who only followed instructions will wait to be told. Make sure your team understands the purpose behind the practice. That is what gives it life after a transition.

5. Build transitions into your Lean system

Do not treat turnover as an interruption. Treat it as part of the work. When someone new joins, make sure they are shown the habits on day one. Walk the board. Join a huddle. Solve a problem. Learn the rhythm. If that is how the team works, the new person adjusts. Not the system.

6. Make standard work part of handoff

When roles change, include process documentation in the transition. Not a binder. Just the basics of what the work looks like now. What is stable. What is improving. What routines matter most. Share the thinking, not just the tasks. That is how continuity lives past the calendar invite.

7. Pay attention right after the change

Transitions are when Lean is most at risk. For thirty days after a role shift, stay close. Watch the routines. Walk the floor. Ask what feels unclear. If a habit starts to fade, reinforce it. Not with pressure. With presence. That is when the system either resets or slips.

You will know your system is attrition-proof when the work stays focused without extra effort. When the routine holds even when the person does not. When Lean is not carried by one voice, but by shared behavior across the team. That is how you make it last. Not by holding on tighter. By building it so it does not need to be held at all.

Reinforce Culture During the Tough Cycles

Every Lean system gets tested. Maybe the numbers slip. Maybe a big customer shifts demand. Maybe the team is short and the pressure is up. Whatever the reason, the moment will come. That is when most systems drift. Not because Lean stopped working. Because leadership stopped showing up for it. Most leaders do not abandon Lean outright. They just start cutting corners. A few huddles get skipped. Visual boards go quiet. Problem solving turns into reaction. People hear things like just do what you have to or we will fix it later. That message spreads fast. It tells the team Lean only matters when it is easy. And once that belief takes hold, it is hard to get back.

Sustaining Lean means holding the line when the pressure shows up. That is what the routines are built for. Not for when things are smooth. For when they are not. You do not protect the system by getting louder. You protect it by staying steady. By making sure the questions do not change. By staying in the work. By keeping the rhythm even when the room gets noisy. This does not mean ignoring business needs. It means responding with discipline. If a deadline moves up, the process does not disappear. If a team is tired, the check-in still happens. If the work shifts, the routines adjust, but they do not go away. The message is clear. We solve problems here. Even now.

You will know the culture is holding when the habits do not slip under pressure. When people still raise problems. When huddles still happen. When the focus stays on process, not panic. That is how you know the culture is real. That is how you know Lean is part of how the team thinks.

Tough cycles do not break a system. They reveal it. If the behavior was built on compliance, it fades. If it was built on belief, it stays. That is the test. And that is where leadership earns its weight. Not through noise. Through presence. Through the choice to hold steady when others would drift. That is what keeps the culture. And that is what makes Lean last.

Know When the System Is Slipping

Lean does not break in one day. It slips. Quietly. Slowly. One routine at a time. The huddle runs long or gets skipped. The board stops getting updated. Problems get mentioned but not solved. People stop asking why. When these things happen, the structure might still be standing, but the system is no longer working.

If you are not watching closely, it is easy to miss. The numbers might still look fine. People might still say the right things. But the energy is off. The rhythm is gone. That is the early signal. And if you wait until the results drop to act, it is already too late. You do not need a dashboard to see it. You need presence. Pay attention to what people talk about. Are they solving problems or explaining them away. Are they asking good questions or avoiding the hard ones. Are the tools helping or just sitting there. These are signs. If the behavior shifts, the system is shifting with it. The job of a Lean leader is not just to start the work. It is to watch for when it starts to fade. And when you see it, you name it. You reset the rhythm. You go back to basics. Not to punish. To remind. You walk the board. You ask what is stuck. You coach the five whys. You bring the habits back through quiet repetition.

You will know the system is coming back when the team stops performing and starts engaging. When the boards show real blockers. When the conversation moves from status to problem solving. That is when the culture is back on track.

Every system drifts. Even the strong ones. What matters is how fast you see it and what you do next. If you lead Lean like a practice, not a project, you will feel it when it slips. And you will know how to bring it back. Simple. Clear. Without drama. That is what real leaders do. That is how Lean stays alive.

Sustain Through Simplicity, Not Scale

Most leaders do not let go of Lean because it failed. They let go because it got too heavy. Too many templates. Too many steps. Too many things that take time but do not change the work. When the system becomes more complicated than the problem it was meant to solve, people stop using it. Simplicity is what sustains. Not less effort. Less noise. The best Lean systems are not the biggest. They are the clearest. A team that runs a solid daily huddle, updates a real visual board, and solves small problems in real time will outperform a team with ten tools they only use when someone is watching.

Simplicity does not mean easy. It means sharp. It means focused. You do fewer things, but you do them well. You protect the habits that matter and let go of the ones that are just there for show. You review the system with the team and ask what adds value. You adjust when needed. Not to be trendy. To stay real.

You will know the system is simple enough when people stop needing to be reminded. When the tools help the work move. When teams can lead it without you. When nothing feels like an extra job. Just the job. That is when you know Lean has become part of the way the work runs.

Lean was never meant to be complex. It was meant to be clear. And when you lead it that way, it holds. Quietly. Consistently. Without needing to be relaunched. Simplicity is not the enemy of rigor. It is the foundation. That is what makes Lean last. Not a bigger system. A better one. One that fits the work. One that people carry forward because it works. Not because they are told. Because they see the value. Every day. That is how you sustain it. And that is how you lead it.

The Research Behind It

Lean systems fail more often from complexity than from lack of effort. That is what the research shows. A study published by the Lean Global Network found that organizations trying to sustain too many tools at once saw a sharp drop in adoption within the first year. The more steps required, the more support needed to keep them moving. And when that support faded, so did the system. The Shingo Institute has long emphasized that the sustainability of any improvement effort depends on principle-based simplicity. Their model reinforces that systems with clear purpose and minimal complexity are more likely to hold during stress, transitions, and leadership changes. It is not about having fewer tools. It is about using the right ones consistently.

Toyota's internal documentation supports this. They did not scale by adding layers. They scaled by anchoring core practices. Daily management. Standard work. Problem solving at the source. These routines were simple, repeatable, and visible. The strength came not from volume but from discipline. James Womack and Dan Jones, in their follow-up Lean studies, also warned that many companies made the mistake of overbuilding Lean. They introduced complicated systems that looked impressive but were hard to maintain. The result was short bursts of improvement followed by a slow slide back to old ways of working.

The evidence is clear. You do not scale Lean by expanding the system. You sustain it by making it fit the work. Keep it visible. Keep it useful. Keep it owned by the people doing the work. That is not soft. That is smart. The best systems are not the most complex. They are the ones that last. Because they are clear. Because they are sharp. Because they help. That is what matters. And that is what the research shows.

In Summary

Sustaining Lean is not about keeping the momentum from the launch. It is about building the kind of leadership system that holds even when the spotlight moves on. This chapter broke down what that really takes. You protect the habits that make Lean work. You build ownership into the team. You use the tools to manage the work, not just track it. And you hold the line when it would be easier to drift.

SUSTAINING THE LEAN TRANSFORMATION

Lean stays alive when leaders make it visible, normal, and nonnegotiable. Not through pressure. Through presence. That presence shows up in the questions you ask, the routines you support, and the systems you refuse to walk away from when the pressure turns up.

You do not need to add more. You need to repeat what already works. Daily huddles. Problem solving at the source. Standard work that keeps the process from slipping. A review rhythm that focuses on learning, not just numbers. These are not Lean extras. These are the foundation. If they stay strong, the system holds. If they slip, everything slips with them. The truth is this. Lean does not fail because the team forgot. It fails because leadership stopped doing the work to protect the behavior. But when leaders keep showing up with discipline and clarity, Lean does not need to be relaunched. It becomes the way the work runs.

That was the focus here. How to keep Lean alive. What comes next is about how to lead it forward.

> The workplace is changing. Technology is accelerating. Data is everywhere. Teams are more distributed. And decision cycles are faster. If Lean is going to stay relevant in this environment, leaders have to adapt without losing what makes Lean strong.

The next chapter is not about trends. It is about how to stay grounded in Lean while using digital tools, data, and systems the right way. It is about leading Lean into what is next. Without noise. Without drift. With focus.

Let's step into that next conversation, Lean Leadership in the Digital Age.

Chapter Fourteen

Lean Leadership in a Digital Age

Lean has always been about seeing the work, solving problems, and creating systems that improve over time. That has not changed. But the environment has. Work is more digital. Teams are more distributed. Decisions move faster. Data shows up before people do. That is the new reality. The challenge is not whether Lean still fits. It does. The challenge is whether leaders are ready to lead it in this new space.

You cannot manage digital work the same way you manage a physical process. You cannot rely on walking the floor when there is no floor to walk. But that does not mean you throw out Lean. It means you adapt the behaviors that make it work. You find new ways to see the work. You use data with discipline. You build routines that stay sharp even when the work is remote or automated.

This chapter is not about digital transformation. It is about leadership. The kind that stays present even when the team is not in the same place. The kind that uses dashboards without losing the human conversation. The kind that keeps Lean focused when everything else is moving faster.

The principles have not changed. Respect for people. Eliminate waste. Solve real problems. But the way those principles show up in practice needs to shift. If you keep leading the same way while the work changes, Lean will start to feel like a thing of the past. But if you stay grounded in the purpose of Lean and smart about how it is applied, it becomes more relevant than ever.

This chapter will show you how to lead Lean when the work is digital, the systems are smarter, and the team is spread out. Not with more tools. With clearer thinking. Let's walk through what that looks like. One habit. One practice. One leadership behavior at a time. That is what keeps Lean alive in a digital world. And that is where we go next.

See the Work When You Cannot See the People

The core of Lean leadership is presence. Not just being available, but being in the work. Seeing it. Asking about it. Supporting it. That was simple when everyone sat together or walked the same floor. But the work has changed. People are remote. Teams are hybrid. The process lives in systems, not in spaces. The risk is obvious. When you cannot see the people, you start losing sight of the work.

You do not fix that by scheduling more meetings. You fix it by being intentional about how you show up. Presence in a digital environment is not about time. It is about rhythm. It is about the habits that keep you close to the work even when the work is not visible.

Start by asking yourself one question. What does it mean to go see in this environment. If your team is remote, go see means logging into the systems they live in. It means sitting in the queue or checking the workflow and watching where things slow down. It means observing how tickets move, how delays form, how handoffs fail. You are not auditing. You are learning.

Replace the hallway check-in with a quick message that asks what slowed you down today. Replace the desk drop-in with a shared board that tells the story in real time. The method changes. The behavior does not.

Keep your questions sharp. What is stuck. What changed. What problem showed up. These are the same questions you would ask walking the floor. Now you ask them in chat, in your huddle, or in a shared comment thread. The goal is not visibility for you. The goal is clarity for the team.

You will know this is working when people stop explaining the tool and start talking about the work. When blockers show up without needing to be chased. When problems are surfaced before results drop. That is not about technology. That is about presence. Lean does not require a physical floor. It requires leaders who know how to see the work. If you cannot walk to it, you log into it. You ask about it. You make it part of your rhythm.

> Digital work will not slow down. But your attention can keep it grounded. You cannot fix what you cannot see. So learn how to see it. Even when no one is in the room. That is the job. And that is what makes Lean work. Even now.

The Research Behind It

Remote and hybrid work is here to stay. That is not opinion. That is what the research says. A 2023 study by McKinsey found that more than 70 percent of companies have adopted a hybrid model in at least one division. Another report from Microsoft's Work Trend Index confirmed that employees now expect flexibility in how and where they work. The world of shared space and fixed hours is not the default anymore. Leadership has to adapt.

The problem is that many Lean habits were built around physical presence. Go see meant walking the floor. Huddles meant gathering around a board. Visual management meant paper and walls. But none of those habits were about the tools. They were about attention. And attention still matters.

Harvard Business Review has shown that teams perform better when they feel their leader is engaged and aware. Not reactive. Not micromanaging. Aware. That awareness drives trust. And trust drives performance. When leaders stop showing up in meaningful ways, distributed teams start to drift.

The Lean Enterprise Institute reinforced this in their post-pandemic review of continuous improvement systems. They found that remote teams who maintained a daily rhythm and had leaders who checked in with purpose were more likely to sustain performance and surface problems early. It was not the tool. It was the behavior behind it.

Amy Edmondson's work on psychological safety also connects here. When people do not feel seen, they stop speaking up. And in digital settings, silence is easy. That is why go see matters more now than ever. You are not walking the floor. You are showing up in the flow. And when you do, the team stays connected.

The research is clear. Digital work does not reduce the need for Lean leadership. It increases it. You cannot lead from distance by default. You lead it by rhythm. By presence. By habits that still ask the right questions. That is what keeps the work aligned. That is what keeps problems visible. And that is what keeps Lean real. Even in a world that is no longer face to face.

Use Data Without Losing the Story

Digital systems give leaders more data than ever. Clicks, cycle times, throughput, satisfaction scores. You can measure almost anything. But more data does not mean better leadership. In fact, when the numbers take over, leaders often stop listening. They start reacting. They use data as proof, not as a prompt. That is when Lean starts to feel like surveillance instead of support.

Lean leaders do not ignore data. They use it the right way. They ask what it shows. They ask what it does not. They look for patterns, not just problems. And they always connect it back to the people doing the work. Data without the story becomes noise. Data with the story becomes focus.

Start with the basics. Pick a few measures that matter. Not everything. Just the ones tied to flow, quality, or customer impact. Make them visible. Make them stable. But do not make them the goal. Make them the signal.

When something changes, ask why. Do not assume. Ask the team. Ask what shifted. Ask what was tried. Ask what the data might be missing. You are not managing from a dashboard. You are managing through it. The dashboard is not the answer. It is the starting point.

Stay alert for false positives. Metrics can look good while the system is slipping. A team can hit cycle time targets while pushing rework downstream. A process can show high completion rates while burying defects. If you do not ask for the story, you will not see the risk. And by the time the data catches up, the damage is already done.

You will know this is working when the team brings you insight, not just numbers. When they explain what the data means without needing to defend it. When metrics drive questions instead of fear. That shift means the system is healthy. It means people trust the process. It means Lean is working the way it should.

Data will not slow down, either. There will always be more of it. Your job is not to chase every trend. Your job is to keep the story intact. That is what makes the numbers useful. And that is what makes leadership real. Not the chart. The thinking behind it. Every time.

The Research Behind It

Leaders have more access to data than ever before. But research shows that more data does not always lead to better decisions. A 2022 report from the *MIT Sloan Management Review* found that over 60 percent of managers feel overwhelmed by the volume of performance data they receive. The problem is not the numbers. It is how they are used. When data becomes the focus, people stop looking at the work. They manage charts, not processes.

Lean has always treated data as a tool for learning, not judgment. W. Edwards Deming said it early. Without theory, data is meaningless. You need context. You need purpose. The best systems use data to test thinking, not to replace it.

The Lean Enterprise Institute's long-term studies show that organizations with strong Lean cultures use fewer metrics, not more. But they use them well. They choose leading indicators tied to process behavior. They discuss them regularly. They link them to actions the team controls. That is what makes the difference. Not how many metrics exist. How many get used to improve the work.

Harvard research on decision quality reinforces this. Leaders who connect data to stories make better decisions. They understand root cause more clearly. They avoid jumping to conclusions. And they build more trust with their teams. When metrics are isolated from the work, they drive fear. When they are paired with narrative, they drive learning.

Amy Edmondson's research on psychological safety adds another layer. In data-heavy environments, safety drops when leaders treat metrics as the only truth. Teams stop reporting problems. They hide variation. The dashboard stays green while the process erodes. But when leaders ask what the numbers mean and invite reflection, safety goes up. People share the truth because they know it will be heard, not punished.

The evidence is clear. Data does not drive improvement on its own. People do. If you want metrics to help, you need leaders who stay curious. You need stories that explain the numbers. You need systems that reward learning, not just hitting the target. That is not soft. That is smart. And that is what makes Lean hold up when the work becomes digital. Data alone is not enough. What matters is how leaders use it. Repeatedly. Thoughtfully. With the people who know the work. That is the system. And that is what lasts.

Keep Problem Solving Real in Virtual Spaces

In a physical space, problem solving often starts with what someone sees or hears. A missed step. A delay. A handoff that did not land. Someone speaks up. They talk it out. They fix it. That kind of rhythm is easier when the team shares space. But now the work is digital. People sit in different places. Systems automate steps. Chat replaces conversation. And the risk is clear. Problems stay buried because the process is out of view.

But Lean does not stop because the work is virtual. It just needs a different kind of leadership. One that keeps problem solving grounded in real issues, even when the team is not in the same room.

Start by naming the problem. Literally. Build a digital space where blockers are called out in plain language. Not tagged. Not coded. Written clearly. What happened. Where it happened. Why it matters. This could be a shared document, a board in your workflow tool, or just a pinned thread in a chat. The format is not the point. The visibility is.

Use short cycles. Run weekly check-ins where the focus is one thing: what is stuck and what has been tried. This is not a report. It is a rhythm. The goal is not to track everything. The goal is to keep real problems in front of the people who can fix them.

Lean tools still work here. The five whys. A3 thinking. Root cause checks. But you have to use them with more intention. You cannot rely on someone watching the room. You have to make the questions part of the habit. Write them down. Talk them through in small groups. Let the team lead it. Remember, your role is to ask, not to answer.

You will know this is working when the problems are specific, not vague. When someone says here is what we think caused it and here is what we tried. When fixes are small and fast, not big and stalled. When the team learns out loud. That is not about technology. That is about discipline.

Problem solving does not need to be in person. It needs to be real. The thinking still applies. The rhythm still matters. What changes is how you show up and how clearly you make the path. If the team knows what to do when something breaks, Lean still lives. Even on a screen. Even across time zones. That is the job. Keep it real. Keep it sharp. Keep it moving.

Lead Standard Work in a System That Changes Fast

Digital systems do not stay still. Updates roll out overnight. Platforms change. New tools get added. Buttons move. Features disappear. That is the environment now. And when that happens, teams scramble to adjust. The risk is not that they fail to adapt. The risk is that they lose what worked. The process breaks, but no one sees it until the impact shows up.

> Standard work is what protects the process from slipping during change. Not as a rulebook. As an anchor. It is not about locking the team into one method. It is about making sure there is a clear starting point when the system shifts. When things move fast, clarity matters more.

Start by defining what good looks like right now. Do not wait for a perfect process. Capture the version that works today. Keep it short. Keep it visual. Keep it close to the work. The goal is not to document everything. The goal is to make it easier to train, to hand off, to recover when the system changes again.

Make it part of the rhythm. When something shifts in the platform, check the standard. Did the update change a step. Did it remove a check. Did it create a new risk. Do not assume. Walk the process again. Ask the team. Update only what needs to change. Leave what still works.

You will know this is working when questions get answered without needing to escalate. When new team members get up to speed faster. When someone flags a system change because it breaks the flow, not just because it feels different. That is the shift. The team owns the standard. They protect it. They adjust it. That is how Lean lives in a system that moves.

Digital tools will keep evolving. That will not stop. But the work still needs to be done right. That means standard work is not extra. It is essential. Not because it limits the team. Because it keeps the process from drifting. Fast systems need strong anchors. That is what standard work gives you. A place to start. A place to return to. A way to hold the gain when everything else moves. That is real leadership. And that is how you lead Lean in digital work.

The Research Behind It

Standard work is not about slowing the team down. It is about keeping them from falling apart when things change. And in digital environments, things change fast. New systems. New updates. New tools. If the team has to figure it out from scratch every time, they will waste energy and create problems that were already solved.

A study in the *International Journal of Operations and Production Management* found that digital teams with basic standard work recovered faster from system changes than those without it. They knew what good looked like. They could spot what broke. They fixed it without guessing. The teams without standard work took longer, made more errors, and needed more help. It was not about more documentation. It was about knowing what had worked and having something to go back to.

Toyota has done this for decades. Even in their digital teams, they update standard work often. Not to add control. To keep clarity. When something in the system changes, the team checks what needs to shift. They fix the standard. Then they move. That rhythm keeps the process stable even when the tools move around them.

James Womack and Daniel Jones saw the same thing. When teams solve problems but never write down what worked, the fix does not hold. Something shifts and the same issue shows up again. That is not progress. That is drift. And drift kills Lean.

McKinsey backed this up in their digital transformation work. Companies with clear but simple process steps adjusted faster to new platforms. Teams knew what to hold onto and what to change. Where that was missing, transitions slowed down the work and introduced more rework. The message was clear. It is not about having a manual. It is about having something the team uses.

The Shingo Institute says the same thing. If you want consistency and alignment, you need a shared view of what good looks like. Standard work gives you that view. And when it is kept fresh, it keeps the system strong.

The research is clear. In fast moving environments, you do not drop standard work. You depend on it. Not to control the team. To give them a place to stand when everything else shifts. That is what protects the system. That is what keeps improvement from slipping. And that is what real leaders reinforce. Quiet. Consistent. Every time.

Coach the Habit, Not the Tool

Digital systems are full of tools. Dashboards. Boards. Notifications. Templates. They are everywhere. But tools do not solve problems. People do. And in a digital environment, it is easy to confuse clicking the tool with doing the work. That is where leadership matters most.

The risk is that teams follow the form but lose the thinking. They fill in an A3 because it is assigned. They click done because the system says to. They check the box but never stop to ask what is broken and why it matters. That is not Lean. That is theater.

> Lean leaders do not coach tools. They coach habits. They ask questions that sharpen the thinking. They push for clarity, not formatting. They know that the value of the five whys is in the conversation, not the bullets. That the value of a visual board is in what it prompts, not what it shows. If the habit is weak, the tool will fail. If the habit is strong, any tool will work.

Start by watching how the team interacts with the work. Not the system. The work. Are they solving problems or just updating status? Are they talking about causes or just reporting outcomes? Are they thinking through issues or waiting for direction? These are signals. If the behavior is shallow, the tool is not the issue.

You fix this by coaching in real time. Ask, what problem are you solving? What made you pick that? What do you expect to change? What will you do next if it does not work? These are not checklist questions. They are leadership questions. They build discipline. They sharpen focus.

You will know this is working when the team starts using the tools to solve problems, not just report them. When they ask for help with the issue, not just with the software. When they come to you with thinking, not just templates. That is the shift. The tool becomes a support. The habit drives the outcome.

The system will keep changing. New platforms will show up. New formats will be rolled out. But if the habit holds, the work will still improve. Lean was never about the tools. It was about how people think and act in the face of problems. Leaders protect that. Not with updates. With questions. Not with control. With clarity.

That is what carries Lean through the noise. That is what keeps it real. Every time.

The Research Behind It

The best Lean systems do not succeed because they picked the right tools. They succeed because leaders coached the right behavior. That is not a theory. That is what the data shows. When tools are introduced without habits, they fade. When habits are built into how people think and work, the system lasts, even when the platform changes.

A study published by the Lean Enterprise Institute found that the most common failure point in Lean adoption was not tool misuse. It was shallow behavior. Teams used the template but did not use the thinking. They updated the board but stopped talking about the blockers. They answered the five whys but did not go past the first one. The form was filled out. The habit was missing.

John Shook said it clearly. Lean is not something you implement. It is something you become. That means coaching how people think, not just what they click. The team has to understand what good problem solving looks like. Not what it looks like in the system. What it looks like in the work.

James Clear, author of *Atomic Habits*, said it another way. You do not rise to the level of your tools. You fall to the level of your habits. If teams do not think critically, no tool will make up for it. But if the thinking is sharp, the format does not matter. That principle applies to Lean just as much as to health or sports or leadership.

Harvard research on behavior change found the same pattern. Systems only hold when the behavior is coached. When people are shown what good looks like and reinforced when they do it. Not through pressure. Through clarity. Through repetition.

Amy Edmondson's work on psychological safety adds another layer. When leaders coach with curiosity instead of control, teams think more clearly. They stop trying to please. They start solving problems. That trust keeps Lean from turning into compliance. It makes the work real.

The research is clear. Tools are helpful. But without habit, they are just noise. Coaching is what makes the system last. Not once. Every time the team starts to drift. Every time the problem gets tricky. Every time someone needs to pause and think.

You do not need more templates. You need better questions. Asked often. Backed by trust. That is how Lean survives the digital shift. That is how it becomes how the work gets done. Not because of the platform. Because of the leadership. And the habit behind it.

Stay Present Without Being Overbearing

When the team works across screens and tools, it is easy for leaders to drift too far out or lean too far in. Some check out and trust the tools to manage. Others jump into every thread and slow the work down. Neither one works. Lean leadership is not passive. It is not controlling. It is present.

Presence does not mean being on every call. It means being in the work just enough to see what matters, support what is stuck, and reinforce the habits that keep the system strong. It means showing up often enough that your absence is noticed. But never so much that your presence is a problem.

Start by setting a rhythm. Pick times to check the board, review the flow, or join a huddle. Show up without warning but never without purpose. Ask sharp questions. What is not moving. What is unclear. What changed. Stay long enough to learn. Then step back.

> Let the team lead. Your role is not to monitor. It is to model. You are not there to fix. You are there to guide. When a problem shows up, ask what they think is causing it. Ask what they have tried. Do not take it from them. Stay curious. Stay steady.

Use the systems to stay close, not to manage. Comments in a shared doc. A check in thread. A tag when something blocks progress. Keep it simple. Keep it real. Let your presence come through in the habits you reinforce, not the volume of messages you send.

You will know this is working when the team starts naming blockers without waiting. When they solve first and update second. When they trust that you will show up when needed but do not wait for you to move. That is the balance. That is the leadership.

Lean does not need louder leaders. It needs leaders who show up with purpose, ask better questions, and let the team own the work. Not from a distance. Not from control. From the right kind of presence. Clear. Trusted. And felt even when the camera is off. That is how Lean holds up. And that is how you lead it.

The Research Behind It

When teams are spread out, leadership presence either builds trust or creates distance. Research from *Harvard Business Review* found that in remote and hybrid environments, what mattered most was not how often leaders showed up, it was how they showed up.

The teams that performed best had leaders who were consistent, clear, and grounded in purpose. They asked better questions. They stayed close to the work. They did not micromanage. They stayed visible without taking control.

Amy Edmondson's research on psychological safety confirms this. Teams need to know their leader will show up, listen, and support action without stepping in to solve it. That kind of presence builds confidence. It tells the team their voice matters. And when they believe that, they start solving problems instead of escalating them.

Microsoft's latest work on hybrid effectiveness supports this too. Employees who felt their leaders were present with purpose, not just sending check ins or watching dashboards, reported higher clarity, better alignment, and more confidence in their daily work. It was not about pressure. It was about rhythm. A leader who showed up with intent, stayed just long enough to understand the work, and trusted the team to move forward was seen as a strong one.

The Lean Enterprise Institute reviewed systems that held up through digital transitions. The ones that worked had one shared trait: leaders did not change their behavior, only their format. Daily huddles still happened. Visual management still existed. Go see became screen share. The structure held because the leadership habit stayed the same.

The Shingo Institute adds to this with their principles of cultural reinforcement. Leaders who engage regularly, ask consistent questions, and stay close to the flow build systems that hold without needing reminders. When presence becomes part of the routine, it keeps Lean alive without turning it into noise.

The research is simple. Presence works when it is steady and useful. Not loud. Not constant. Just visible, honest, and grounded in action. The leader sets the tone. When that tone is built on showing up to learn, not to control, teams respond. And Lean lasts.

That is not a theory. That is what the data says. That is what real leadership looks like. And that is how you keep the system strong when everything else is moving. Quiet. Consistent. Present.

Protect Lean Thinking When the Tech Promises to Solve Everything

Digital systems are built to make things easier. Faster approvals. Cleaner data. Fewer manual steps. That sounds good. But the risk is that leaders start thinking the system will do the thinking for them. They stop asking what is causing delays or where the waste lives.

They stop watching the process. They trust the tool to catch what is wrong and forget how to see it for themselves.

Lean does not work that way. You do not outsource the thinking. You sharpen it. You use the system, but you never let it replace your questions. If the tool says the work is on track but the process still feels broken, you go look. If the chart says quality is holding but the team is raising issues, you ask why. The system gives you data. The thinking makes sense of it.

> You protect Lean thinking by teaching people to stay curious even when the numbers look good. Ask where the data comes from. Ask how it gets updated. Ask what it hides. Not to question the tool. To stay grounded in the work.

You also make sure the team does not stop thinking. If a metric shows green, ask what it means. Ask what changed. Ask what might shift it again. When a dashboard replaces a board, make sure it still prompts the right conversations. If it becomes a wall of numbers no one uses, it is noise.

You will know you are protecting Lean thinking when the system is treated like a tool, not a decision maker. When people still walk the process. When leaders still ask the five whys. When metrics are used to start learning, not end the conversation. That is the difference.

Digital systems are helpful. But they do not solve problems. People do. And the moment leaders stop thinking that way, the system becomes the focus instead of the work. Lean does not break because a tool was added. It breaks when the thinking stops. That is what you protect. That is what keeps it real. And that is the work. Every time.

Back in my day. An author reflection.

Back in my day, I was working with a software company on the East Coast, that had just rolled out a new support platform. The tool came with everything: automated ticket routing, live dashboards, and alerts that flagged issues before anyone asked. Leadership was convinced it was going to clean everything up. Faster resolution. Fewer escalations. Better customer experience. On paper, it looked great.

A few weeks in, the metrics backed that up. Tickets closed faster. The backlog shrank. Satisfaction scores edged up. But when we sat with the support team, the tone changed. One rep said, "We close tickets fast because the system tells us to. Not because they are fixed." Another said the automation was moving tickets through without solving the real problem. It looked clean. It was not.

When we looked deeper, it turned out the team was chasing numbers instead of fixing the work. The system sorted tickets by rules, not by context. So people responded based on what the system surfaced, not what actually mattered. And no one was asking what caused the issues in the first place. The tool did not stop them from thinking. It replaced the need to think.

I asked one of the supervisors what they were doing to improve the process. He looked at me and said, "We are not. The software handles it now."

That is the risk. The system looked like it was working. But the team had checked out. They were reacting to the tool, not leading through the work. The leaders were reading dashboards. They were not walking the process. Nobody was asking why. Nobody was fixing root causes.

We pulled them back. No resets. No big push. Just a few focused steps. Mapped the support flow. Asked the five questions. Found the gaps that the tool had hidden. And we made it clear, if the numbers say green and the people doing the work say red, *you trust the people*.

It took a few months, but the shift happened. The team started speaking up again. Problems started getting fixed, not passed along. The tool stayed. But the thinking returned. That is what mattered.

Digital systems can help. But they cannot think. And when leaders start trusting the system more than the people, Lean slips. The work starts to look right, even when it is wrong. Your job is to keep the questions alive. Stay in the process. Trust what you hear. That is what keeps Lean real. Especially when the screen says everything is fine.

Use Technology to Amplify, Not Replace, the Right Habits

Technology can help you see more. Track more. Respond faster. But only if the habits are already in place. If the team is not solving problems today, software will not make them start. If leaders are not asking the right questions, a dashboard will not ask them for you. If huddles do not happen, adding a digital board will not change anything.

Lean works because of the behavior. The rhythm. The focus. When a team solves problems in real time, a tracking tool makes that easier. When a leader shows up with purpose, a shared board makes the conversation faster. When the habits are strong, technology helps. But when the habits are missing, the system becomes noise.

Use tools to reinforce what you want more of. If you want better huddles, make blockers visible on a shared board. If you want ownership, let the team update metrics and call out issues. If you want more problem solving, add a space where the five whys can be tracked and tested. Do not let the tool run the habit. Let the habit shape how the tool is used.

You will know it is working when the tool disappears behind the work. When the conversation is about the problem, not the platform. When the team still meets, still thinks, still solves, whether the tool is open or not. That is the sign. Lean is not being driven by software. It is being supported by it.

That is the goal. You do not need more automation. You need more alignment. If the tool helps with that, use it. If it gets in the way, fix the process first. Then bring the system along. Not the other way around.

Technology is not the solution. It is just a tool. The real solution is the behavior it supports. Keep that sharp. Keep it simple. And let the tool follow the work. Not lead it.

The Research Behind It

Studies across industries continue to show the same truth. Technology does not change behavior. It amplifies it. The Lean Enterprise Institute found that in companies where daily management, problem solving, and coaching habits were already strong, digital tools improved performance. But in companies where those habits were missing, adding software did nothing. Or worse, it made the gaps harder to see.

McKinsey's work on digital transformation backs that up. They found that more than seventy percent of tech-driven improvement efforts failed to deliver results. Not because the tools did not work, but because the teams never changed how they worked. The platform got smarter. The process did not. And without process discipline, the tech became a distraction.

Toyota's approach has been consistent. They do not chase software. They build strong habits first. Visual management. Standard work. Problem solving. Then they layer in systems to make those behaviors easier to repeat. The tech never replaces the habit. It supports it. And that is why it works.

A Harvard study on workflow automation showed that systems designed to reduce manual tasks only improved outcomes when paired with strong team routines. Without those routines, the systems introduced more rework. The work got done faster. But it was the wrong work.

The Shingo Institute highlights the same thing. Their research on principle-driven systems shows that operational excellence only holds when behaviors are anchored in purpose. Tools may help, but they do not drive the culture. The habits do. If the tools are added without strong purpose, they fade. Or worse, they get misused.

The pattern is clear. You do not start with the system. You start with the behavior. If the habit is real, the tool helps. If the habit is weak, the tool hides the problem.

Leaders who get this right do not look for better platforms. They build better habits. Then they use tech to make those habits easier to sustain. Not louder. Sharper. And that is what the research supports. That is what holds the system together. And that is the work. Every day. Done with discipline. Backed by action. Never by automation alone.

Close the Gaps Between Tech, Process, and People

Digital tools are built to support work. But if you are not careful, they start replacing the connection between people and process. The system says a task is done, but no one has confirmed it. The board shows green, but the team is still stuck. The workflow looks perfect, but nobody trusts it.

This happens when leaders do not check what the system hides. It happens when the tool is treated like the process instead of a way to see it. It also happens when teams are expected to follow steps that no longer reflect the way the work is actually done.

> Your job is to close that gap. Start by asking simple questions. Does this tool match the way we do the work today? Do the people using it trust what it shows? Do we still talk about what is broken, or do we just update the screen? If those answers do not feel clear, the system needs to change. Not the conversation.

Go walk the process. Compare what the system shows with what is really happening. Ask the team where they click just to move forward. Ask what steps are skipped or added. If the workflow does not match the work, fix the process first. Then update the tool.

You will know this is working when the system reflects the process instead of distorting it. When blockers in the work show up in the workflow. When leaders stop needing reports because they can see what matters. That is when the gaps close. And that is what keeps the system real.

Digital systems can help. But they cannot lead. That is your job. Stay close. Ask the questions. Fix what does not match. The board is not the process. The person is. And the better you close that gap, the stronger your Lean system becomes. Not because of the tool. Because of the trust built around it. Every day. Repeated. Grounded in what is real.

The Research Behind It

Research from MIT Sloan shows that digital transformation efforts fail most often when technology is layered over broken or outdated processes. The system gets smarter. The confusion gets faster. This disconnect leads to increased complexity, not better performance. Teams spend more time explaining the tool than fixing the work.

A study published by McKinsey found that in organizations where digital systems did not align with actual work practices, productivity dropped. Leaders believed they were creating efficiency. Employees said the tools created more friction. That friction slowed problem solving and buried the truth under layers of system noise.

The Lean Enterprise Institute has tracked similar results. In environments where visual boards, huddles, and process reviews were tied directly to actual work, performance held steady even as new platforms were introduced. But in places where teams updated systems without reviewing the real process, rework increased. Engagement fell. Ownership disappeared. The system was active. The work was not.

Harvard research into digital workflows showed that process mismatches create quiet risk. Workarounds increase. Trust in the data drops. Communication fades. This leads to a culture where people stop saying what is wrong because the system says everything is fine. By the time the metrics show a problem, the damage is already done.

Toyota's development approach reinforces this idea. They do not automate what is unclear. They clarify the work first. They test the flow. They refine the process. Then they apply the tool. If the tool ever stops matching the process, they update the tool. Never the other way around.

James Clear's work on behavior systems points to the same principle. Your results are not just based on the goals you set. They are shaped by the systems you follow. If the system does not match the habit, the habit will not last. If the habit is strong but the system makes it harder, the habit breaks down.

The pattern is clear. When tools are built to match the process and the process reflects the reality of the work, Lean systems hold. When those connections slip, the system starts to drift. Trust fades. Ownership disappears. You do not fix that with reminders. You fix it by walking the process and closing the gap.

That is what the research says. That is what real leaders do. They keep the system grounded. They keep the process real. And they make sure people trust what they see. Not because it is in the system. Because it matches the work. Every time.

Build Digital Awareness Into Lean Coaching

Lean coaching does not stop because the team works across screens. But it does get harder. You cannot read the room the same way. You cannot glance at the board to see if something is stuck. You cannot catch that moment when someone hesitates before speaking. What you lose in visibility, you have to gain back in discipline.

That means asking sharper questions. Listening longer. Noticing silence. Coaching in a digital environment is not about checking in more. It is about making each question do more work. What changed. What got in the way. What have you tried. What would make it better. These are not soft questions. They are sharp tools. And they are even more important when the work is not happening in the same room.

You also have to teach the team how to surface what is real. Ask them what is not being tracked. Ask what is missing from the dashboard. Ask where the system says things are fine but the work tells a different story. Then coach them to close that gap. Not with a better update. With better thinking.

Write it down. Use shared notes. Track decisions. Share what was tried and what was learned. These are not reports. These are learning moments. The more you make the thinking visible, the more the team builds the habit of slowing down and working through problems instead of reporting around them.

You will know this is working when coaching sounds like conversation, not status. When the team starts asking each other what they have tried. When they come to you with thinking instead of requests. You will know it is working when progress keeps happening even when the camera is off. Because the habits are built. And the thinking holds.

Digital work changes the format. Not the responsibility. You still coach. You still ask. You still lead. And the questions still matter. Maybe now more than ever. That is what keeps the system sharp. That is what keeps the culture alive. Not just the tools. The coaching behind them. Done with purpose. Backed by habit. No shortcuts. Just the work. Every time.

Close with Clarity: Keep the Thinking Human in a Digital World

Technology will keep moving. Tools will change. Platforms will update. That is not the problem. The problem is when leaders let those changes replace the thinking that makes Lean work. The problem is when the system looks clean, but the team is quiet. When the dashboard is full, but the process is drifting.

Digital systems can support Lean. But they cannot think. They cannot see what does not add value. They cannot ask what is missing or what feels harder than it should. Only people do that. Only leaders who stay close. Only teams that feel safe to speak up.

If you want Lean to last in a digital world, you have to protect what makes it human. The habits. The questions. The coaching. The shared responsibility. These are not technical skills. They are leadership skills. And they show up in how you act, not what you install.

You will know it is working when the team solves problems before you ask. When metrics drive learning, not compliance. When your presence shapes behavior, even if you are not in the room. That is not an app. That is leadership. Quiet. Present. Consistent.

The next chapter will push further into this reality. It is not about systems. It is about people. How they think. How they feel. And what they do when no one is watching. Let's get into how to lead that. Not with more tools. With more clarity. The human side of digital leadership starts there.

The Research Behind It

Harvard research shows that when leaders rely too much on digital dashboards and system reports, team engagement drops. The systems make things visible, but they also create distance. People stop sharing problems. They stop thinking through the work. They wait for the system to tell them what is wrong. That is when Lean starts to fade.

MIT studies found the same thing. Digital tools helped performance only when leaders used them to support conversations. Not replace them. When tools became the focus, teams stopped asking why. They stopped checking the process. They managed the screen, not the work.

The Lean Enterprise Institute has studied organizations that made Lean last. The pattern was clear. When leaders coached regularly, asked what was missing, and stayed in the process, the habits held, even in remote settings. When leaders backed off and let the tools run the system, improvement slowed. People stopped solving problems. They started reporting around them.

Amy Edmondson's work on psychological safety confirms this. Teams need to feel safe to speak up. Digital tools do not create that safety. Leaders do. If the environment feels like it is just tracking activity, people go quiet. When the conversation stays active, the culture stays strong.

Gartner's latest workplace study found that high performing digital teams used platforms to keep their habits visible. They did not stop running huddles. They did not stop reviewing the work. They used the tools to support what already worked. That is why the results held. Not because the tool was better. Because the behavior was strong.

This is the difference. Technology can help. But it does not lead. And when the thinking gets replaced by a screen, the system starts to slip. Slowly. Quietly. Until people are just checking boxes.

The research is not complex. It says what you already know. Tools help when the habits are strong. Tools hurt when they replace them. Lean does not hold because the software was smart. It holds because the thinking stayed sharp. The leadership stayed close. And the behavior stayed honest. That is what matters. That is what lasts.

In Summary

The truth is Lean will always face pressure. New systems. Changing priorities. Leadership turnover. The day to day noise never stops. And no matter how strong your habits are or how clear your routines become, there will be moments when the system gets tested. Something will push back. A leader will question the time. A team will lose energy. A result will not come fast enough. That is when Lean is most at risk. Not when the tools are missing. When the support starts to fade. Sustaining Lean takes more than discipline. It takes resilience. And resilience is built by how you respond when the system gets hard to protect. The next chapter focuses on that. Not how to avoid resistance, but how to lead through it. With clarity. With purpose. With enough presence to hold the line when others start to drift. That is what real Lean leadership looks like. Let's walk through how to lead when the pushback comes. Because it will. And that is when your leadership matters most.

Chapter Fifteen

Overcoming Challenges and Resistance

If you lead with Lean long enough, you will hit resistance. Not just from skeptics. From smart people. From teams that have seen things fail before. From leaders who support it in theory but hesitate when the pressure shows up. From systems that were not built to change. This is normal. It does not mean Lean is broken. It means you are doing it for real.

Every Lean system runs into friction. The habits take time. The questions slow people down. The focus on process feels uncomfortable when everyone wants results fast. But if you are not prepared to lead through that pushback, the system will not hold. Not because people are against it. Because the pull of old habits is strong.

This chapter is about what to expect and how to lead when Lean starts to get heavy. It is not about avoiding resistance. It is about understanding where it comes from and responding in a way that keeps the culture strong. You do not need to argue. You do not need to convince. You need to lead with presence, stay close to the work, and let the system speak through results.

We will walk through the common sources of resistance, how to respond without backing down, and what to do when the habits start slipping. This is where the real work begins. Not launching Lean. Keeping it alive when others start to question if it is worth it.

Let's get into what that looks like. Clear. Steady. No pushback big enough to shake the system when the leadership behind it stays grounded. That is how you overcome resistance. And that is what this chapter is here to teach.

Understand Where Resistance Comes From

Most resistance to Lean does not come from bad attitudes. It comes from experience. People have seen programs come and go. They have been asked to give input, only to see nothing change. They have sat through training that sounded good but never matched the way the work actually runs. When Lean shows up, they are not fighting the ideas. They are protecting themselves from more disappointment.

You will hear things like, we tried that before. Or, this is just the flavor of the month. Sometimes people say nothing at all. They just nod, smile, and wait for it to go away. That silence is not agreement. It is learned patience. They have seen this movie before. And they know how it usually ends.

The other kind of resistance is quieter. It comes from discomfort. Lean exposes problems. It asks people to look at broken systems, to talk about gaps, and to change habits that feel safe. That is not easy. Even when people agree with the purpose, the process feels like risk. They are not saying no to improvement. They are reacting to the pressure that comes with it.

If you want to lead through resistance, stop taking it personally. Start listening for the truth behind the words. When someone pushes back, ask where it is coming from. Ask what happened last time. Ask what feels hard about this one. You are not trying to convince them. You are trying to understand what they see.

> Do not argue. Do not defend the program. Just name what is real. Say things like, I get why you are hesitant. We have not always followed through before. Or, this change is uncomfortable. I feel that too. That honesty earns more trust than any plan.

You also need to make the first steps feel manageable. Big launches trigger big reactions. Start with one habit. One board. One conversation. Make the first improvement visible. Let the team experience progress instead of hearing about it. That is how belief starts to shift.

You will know you are handling resistance the right way when people start raising concerns earlier and more directly. Not because they are trying to block you. Because they trust you enough to say what they think. That is the opening. That is where the change starts.

Do not avoid resistance. Do not ignore it. Walk straight into it. Ask the questions that bring it forward. Then lead through it with action, not pressure. The resistance is not the threat. Silence is. And the way to beat it is not with more energy. It is with presence, patience, and a willingness to listen before you lead. That is what earns support. That is what turns doubt into movement. One conversation at a time. Repeated. Grounded. And backed by what happens next.

The Research Behind It

Resistance to Lean is not usually about the tools. It is about trust. Research from McKinsey found that seventy percent of transformation efforts fail, and one of the top reasons is skepticism created by past experiences. People do not resist because they are negative. They resist because they have learned that change often means more work with less follow through. The problem is not the content. It is the memory of what did not work last time.

The Lean Enterprise Institute reinforces this. In long term case studies, they found that the most successful Lean efforts began with small, visible changes that built credibility before asking for broad adoption. In contrast, efforts that started with full scale rollouts often met quiet resistance and low engagement. The teams had seen big efforts launch before. They were waiting to see if this one would last.

Harvard Business Review published findings that linked resistance to psychological safety. When teams felt safe to speak openly and share concerns, resistance dropped and engagement increased. But in organizations where concerns were dismissed or avoided, resistance grew. Even when the leaders were well intentioned, ignoring pushback signaled that input was not welcome.

Edgar Schein's work on organizational culture confirms this. Culture is not shaped by new language or new systems. It is shaped by how leaders respond when people question the direction. If the reaction is pressure or defense, resistance hardens. If the reaction is curiosity and respect, trust builds.

The Shingo Institute also emphasizes that behavior leads belief. When people see consistent action, their attitude follows. But when they are asked to change before they see anything different, they disengage. The credibility gap becomes the barrier. And the only way through it is repetition of real change, not more explanation.

The research is consistent. You do not overcome resistance with better messaging. You overcome it by understanding what people have lived through and showing them something different this time. Not once. Repeated. With fewer promises and more proof.

That is not theory. That is leadership. That is how you earn trust. And that is what makes Lean real. Not because you said it would be. Because you showed it. Consistently. And the team could feel the difference.

Lead Through Doubt Without Forcing Buy-In

Not everyone will buy in on day one. That is fine. You do not need everyone to believe right away. You need them to see something real. Most leaders make the mistake of trying to convince everyone first. They explain the benefits. They roll out a vision. They ask for commitment before there is anything to commit to. That is backwards. Buy-in does not come from the kickoff. It comes from what happens next.

> When people doubt Lean, do not fight it. Do not push harder. Just start the work. Show what it looks like when the system is working. Let the team see one blocker removed. One problem solved. One habit that actually helps instead of adds noise. That is what shifts belief. Not the pitch. The proof.

You are not looking for permission. You are building credibility. That means you do not need everyone on board to start. You need one or two people willing to try. Support them. Make the change visible. Let others watch. Most teams do not need more explanation. They need a reason to believe this time is different. That only comes when they see the work get better.

Lead with action. Talk less about Lean and more about what is not working in the current process. Ask what slows people down. Ask what feels harder than it should. Then fix one of those things. Keep the change small. Keep the feedback tight. Let people speak up. Let them see it happen.

Do not try to win the skeptics. Just keep showing up with respect. Keep asking what is broken. Keep fixing what you can with the people who are ready. The rest will come when they stop hearing Lean and start seeing results.

You will know it is working when the tone shifts. When people start saying, that made a difference. When they start asking to join instead of being told to. When they stop testing the words and start watching the behavior. That is buy-in. Not from pressure. From proof.

You do not need to push belief. You need to lead through doubt with calm, steady action. If Lean is real, it will show up in the work. And when it does, people follow. Not because they were told to. Because they want to. That is the difference. And that is how you lead through doubt. Quiet. Present. Real. Repeated until the work speaks for itself.

The Research Behind It

Harvard research on organizational change shows that early adoption is rarely driven by belief. It is driven by observation. When people see results, they participate. When they are asked to support something that has not delivered yet, they wait. That waiting is not resistance. It is rational. They want to see if the effort is worth their trust.

The Lean Enterprise Institute studied dozens of organizations that implemented Lean over multiple years. The data showed that leaders who focused on proving value through small, real improvements gained broader support over time. Leaders who led with declarations or large-scale rollouts saw more skepticism and slower adoption. The message was clear. People trust what they see, not what they are told.

Amy Edmondson's research on psychological safety reinforces this. When leaders push for commitment before teams feel safe to engage, they create pressure instead of momentum. But when leaders lead with curiosity, solve a problem, and make it visible, trust increases. The change starts to feel real. That is when people lean in.

Studies from McKinsey found that transformation efforts with a strong "early proof" model; where pilot teams solved one issue visibly created faster scaling. They did not rely on companywide belief. They relied on what worked. One team. One fix. One win. Repeated.

This matches decades of insight from Toyota. The company never pushed for buy-in. They taught by doing. One improvement. One problem solved. The belief followed the action. The phrase they used was simple. Go see. Fix what is real. Let people witness the change.

The research is consistent. You do not win belief first. You earn it. You lead by doing the work. You keep the change small. You stay close to the process. And when people see that it helps, not in theory, but in the work, they get on board. Not because of the words. Because of the outcome.

That is what makes Lean take hold. That is what makes it stick. The proof comes first. The belief comes next. And the leader sets the pace. Not with pressure. With presence. Every time.

Respond When Habits Start to Slip

Lean does not fail in a day. It slips. A huddle gets skipped. A board does not get updated. A problem is spotted but no one asks why. At first, it feels small. The numbers still look good. The team still sounds aligned. But something is off. The rhythm is gone.

When Lean habits slip, do not wait. Do not assume it will fix itself. And do not overreact. You are not correcting the team. You are resetting the routine. That starts with visibility. Show up. Go to the board. Ask what is stuck. Ask why the update is missing. Ask what changed. Not to call someone out. To bring the habit back into focus.

Most of the time, the cause is simple. The meeting ran long. The workload shifted. A new person was not trained on the routine. No one decided to stop. It just happened. That is what makes the slip dangerous. Because if you let it slide, it sends a message. The habit is optional. That is when the culture starts to shift back.

You do not need a new rollout. You need a reset. Quiet. Direct. Reinforce the behavior. Join the huddle. Help with the board. Coach the five whys. Ask what happened. Ask what is next. The goal is not to punish. The goal is to remind. The system works when the behavior holds. That is the standard.

You will know the reset worked when the habit starts running without you again. When people return to the routine without pushback. When someone else notices a slip and calls it out before you do. That is the sign the culture is holding.

> Lean will drift. Every system does. The test is how fast you catch it and what you do next. Not through a speech. Through presence. Through small corrections. Through daily reinforcement that the habits still matter.

Do not wait until the numbers fall. Watch the behavior. And when the rhythm is off, get it back. Quickly. Calmly. Repeatedly. That is how you lead a system that lasts. Not with pressure. With discipline. Every day. Even when no one is watching. Especially then.

The Research Behind It

The Lean Enterprise Institute has studied systems that faded after strong starts. The pattern is clear. The drop does not begin with strategy. It begins with habit. Daily huddles get skipped. Visual boards stop getting updated. Problem solving becomes passive. No one decides to abandon Lean. They just stop doing the parts that made it work.

James Clear, in his work on behavior and habit, explains that systems do not fail because of poor intent. They fail because of neglected routine. His research showed that when habits are not reinforced, they fade. Not immediately. Slowly. The structure is still there, but the behavior behind it is gone. That is when results slip.

Toyota's internal studies showed the same. They measured the stability of their production system by tracking routine adherence. When go see visits dropped or leader standard work was skipped, problem solving dropped too. Not because the team lacked skill. Because the rhythm disappeared. When the rhythm went, so did the culture.

Harvard Business Review published a study showing that process adherence starts to drop when the feedback loop disappears. If the board is not used to make decisions, people stop updating it. If the huddle becomes just a checklist, the team stops showing up ready to solve. When the behavior does not feel like it matters, it fades. That is not resistance. That is drift.

The research is consistent. The best systems are not held together by training. They are held together by repetition. The leader sets the tone. When something slips and the leader steps in quickly and calmly to reset the habit, the culture stays strong. When the leader waits or stays quiet, the slip becomes the new normal.

You do not need more meetings. You need more presence. You do not need to change the system. You need to keep the behavior sharp. The research is clear. Drift is natural. Recovery is leadership. That is what protects Lean. And that is what keeps it real.

Stay Grounded When Results Take Time

Lean takes time. Not everything shows up in a report right away. You fix a process. You train the team. You build a new habit. And for a while, the numbers might not move. That does not mean the work is wrong. It means it is real. Any system worth keeping takes more than a few weeks to prove itself. And if you expect results too fast, you will break the rhythm trying to chase them.

This is where most leaders slip. They start strong. The board goes up. The huddles run. People feel the momentum. Then someone asks about results. The leader starts pressing. The team starts performing. Problems get hidden. Updates start to sound good instead of honest. And Lean becomes noise instead of clarity.

Do not rush it. Stay with the work. Ask what changed, not just what moved. Ask what was learned, not just what was finished. Show the team that the right behavior matters more than fast answers. That message is what gives them room to focus on the work instead of managing impressions.

> Be honest with your expectations. Say it straight. This is going to take time. The early work is about building muscle. The results will follow. And when they do, they will hold because the foundation is strong.

Track progress that matters. Did the team test a countermeasure? Did they remove a step? Did they update the standard? That is progress. You do not need every fix to show up in a chart this month. You need to see the team thinking and acting with discipline. That is what leads to results that last.

You will know the system is growing when the team brings you updates without needing to be asked. When they are proud of the problems they solved. When the rhythm holds even when the pressure shows up. That is the signal. The team is not reacting. They are leading. And they trust you to let the work speak for itself.

Do not let urgency break the system. Stay grounded. Keep the habits steady. And remind everyone that Lean works best when it is built right, not rushed. That is what creates a culture that performs. Not in spikes. In seasons. Durable. Trusted. Proven. That is what matters most.

The Research Behind It

Research from the Lean Enterprise Institute shows that the most successful Lean transformations often take twelve to eighteen months before the full impact shows up in measurable results. In the early phases, the changes are happening in behavior, not in charts. Teams are learning to see problems, talk honestly, and solve without fear. That work builds the foundation. But it takes time. When leaders get impatient and push for numbers too soon, the system bends. And it usually breaks.

McKinsey research backs this up. They studied hundreds of improvement efforts across sectors. The difference between those that sustained and those that faded was not strategy. It was patience. Leaders who stayed close to the work and focused on behavior before results had higher long term gains. Those who pushed for fast returns created pressure that forced teams to fake progress and hide problems.

James Womack and Daniel Jones, in their follow-up work on Lean implementation, wrote that real Lean systems do not deliver results in the first quarter. They deliver capability. When capability builds, the results come. But if the system is judged too early, it never gets the chance to work. That is not a failure of Lean. That is a failure of leadership discipline.

Amy Edmondson's research on psychological safety explains why this happens. When teams feel rushed to show success, they protect themselves. They stop experimenting. They stop sharing problems. They say what they think leaders want to hear. That blocks the learning. And when learning stops, the system stalls.

Toyota's internal practices reflect this mindset. Their leaders never chase quick wins. They look for stability in the process before they ask for performance. If the behavior is right, the result will come. If the behavior is forced, the result will not last. That discipline is what makes their system consistent through any cycle.

The research is clear. You do not get lasting results by pushing for speed. You get them by protecting the habits that create the right conditions. You let the team solve real problems. You let the culture take root. And you trust that when the foundation is built, the results will follow. Not all at once. But in a way that holds. That is what makes Lean work. That is what keeps it real. And that is what the best leaders do. Every time.

Turn Early Wins Into Proof, Not Pressure

Early wins matter. But only if you treat them the right way. Too often, leaders take one improvement and turn it into a case study. They package it up, put it in a slide deck, and start telling every team to copy it. That kills momentum. What started as a good thing becomes pressure. The story gets polished. The team stops learning. And other teams start pulling back. Not because the win was wrong. Because the way it was handled made people feel like they were next in line for judgment, not support.

If you want early wins to build belief, do not turn them into a show. Keep them real. Keep them small. Share what changed. Share what was learned. Share what still needs work. That honesty builds trust. And trust is what spreads Lean, not celebration.

Let the team that made the change tell the story. Keep it short. What was the problem? What did they try? What happened? That is enough. No branding. No pitch. Just the truth. The power is not in how impressive the change sounds. It is in how real it feels.

Other teams do not need to be told to do the same thing. They need to be asked what problems they see. What friction they face. Then they need the space to try. The early win is not a template. It is proof that improvement is possible. That is the message.

You will know you are handling early wins the right way when other teams ask, how did they do that. When people start looking at their own work differently. When small improvements become normal instead of news.

Lean does not grow from one big breakthrough. It grows from the belief that change is possible. That belief comes from seeing someone else solve something real without waiting for permission. If your early win becomes proof of that, it will spread. If it becomes pressure to perform, it will stall.

> Protect the tone. Let the work speak. Let the story stay real. That is how you turn one small step into something bigger. Not by pushing harder. By staying steady. That is what makes Lean believable. And that is what makes it last.

The Research Behind It

Research from Harvard Business School shows that early wins are a strong predictor of long term engagement, but only when they are shared as learning, not mandates. When a success is framed as "look what we figured out," it builds energy. When it is framed as "now everyone must do this," it creates resistance. The same result. Two different messages. Only one builds momentum.

The Lean Enterprise Institute studied transformation efforts across industries. In systems that sustained Lean, early wins were used to tell real stories. What worked. What failed. What was adjusted. That built trust. The teams who followed saw the proof, not the pressure. In systems that faded, early wins were polished too fast. They became models instead of milestones. Teams saw them as the new standard to live up to. That shut down learning.

Amy Edmondson's work on psychological safety gives this context. She found that when teams feel like every win will be put under a spotlight, they stop trying. The stakes feel too high. But when wins are shared with transparency and the goal is learning, more teams experiment. More ideas get tested. And the system gets stronger.

James Womack and Daniel Jones wrote that Lean spreads through habit, not hype. They warned that treating early results as success stories can trigger the wrong behaviors. Leaders start demanding replication instead of encouraging discovery. Teams start copying instead of learning. The focus shifts from solving problems to meeting expectations.

Toyota teaches the same principle. One improvement proves that something can be better. It does not mean every other team should make the same change. The win is not the outcome. The win is the method. If the behavior was sound and the thinking was clear, the improvement matters. Even if it was small.

The research is clear. Early wins are valuable. But only if they stay grounded. When the story is honest, when the team owns the learning, and when the focus stays on progress, not perfection, those wins build belief. That belief is what spreads Lean. That belief is what holds the culture. And that is how systems grow without forcing them. One win. Shared with care. Repeated the right way. That is what works. Every time.

Keep Lean Grounded When Leadership Changes

Lean often survives the launch. What it struggles with is the handoff. A leader leaves. A new one steps in. Priorities change. Energy shifts. What used to feel clear starts to feel uncertain. Routines go quiet. Habits get skipped. And the culture that was building starts to stall. Not because people stopped believing. Because no one knows what comes next.

The best systems are not built on personalities. They are built on habits. If Lean only works when one person is in charge, then it was never a system. It was a project. And when that person moves on, the system does too.

Your job is to make sure that does not happen. That starts before the change. Lock in the routines. Make sure the team owns the habits. Daily huddles. Visual boards. Standard work. Coaching. These should not belong to the leader. They should belong to the work. When that is true, the habits hold, even if the name on the door changes.

During a leadership shift, keep the message simple. We are not starting over. We are protecting what works. Reinforce the core behaviors. Show the new leader what is in place and why it matters. Do not try to sell it. Let the habits speak. Let the team show that the system runs without pressure.

You will know it is working when the handoff feels quiet. When the rhythm continues. When the team helps the new leader get up to speed without needing to rebuild from scratch. That is not luck. That is strength. That is what real Lean systems look like.

Leaders will come and go. That is normal. What should not change is how the work gets done. If the system is solid, the routine holds. If the culture is clear, the habits stay. That is what you lead. Not the spotlight. The structure. And when that structure stays steady, so does the performance. No matter who is in the role. That is the point. That is the work.

Back in my day. An author reflection.

Back in my day, I was working with an insurance company back east. They had made solid progress with Lean. Daily huddles were happening. Visual boards were active. Team leads were solving small problems on their own. It was not perfect, but it was working. People were engaged. The work was moving. The system had rhythm.

Then the site leader got promoted. New role. New location. A replacement came in from outside the organization. Sharp. Experienced. But new to Lean. The first few weeks were quiet. Then things started to drift. The huddle was pushed for a staff meeting. The board stopped getting updated. The team stopped raising blockers because they were not sure if it still mattered. It was not sabotage. It was uncertainty. And uncertainty always pulls culture backward.

The system had been built around the leader. Not through bad intent. Just habit. The routines were strong, but they had not become fully owned by the team. So when the leader changed, so did the behavior.

We worked with the new leader to reset. Not with a kickoff. Not with a mandate. Just quiet presence. Ten minutes at the board. One blocker solved. One question asked. We reminded the team that the habits were theirs, not the leader's. The reset worked because we focused on rhythm, not roles.

That experience stayed with me. It proved that Lean cannot live in one person's effort. It has to live in the work. If the routine is owned by the team, leadership changes do not shake it. If the system is fragile, the smallest shift knocks it off course.

You do not prevent turnover. You build systems that hold through it. That is the difference between activity and culture. And that is what makes Lean last.

Make the Case Again When the Context Changes

Lean does not stay safe just because it worked last year. Priorities change. Budgets tighten. New leaders arrive. Something urgent pulls attention. And suddenly, Lean starts feeling like extra instead of essential. This does not mean the effort failed. It means the context changed. And when the context changes, you have to make the case again.

You do not start over. You do not relaunch. You go back to what Lean actually did. What problems were solved. What waste was removed. What results held. Then you walk into the room with that truth. Not a pitch. Not a presentation. Just facts. Grounded. Clear. Honest.

You remind people what Lean prevents. Not just what it improves. The delays that no longer exist. The errors that stopped. The burnout that dropped when the process was fixed. These are not just wins. They are risks that are no longer active. That is the value.

When urgency shows up, it is tempting to pull attention away from the routines. Leaders want to move fast. Skip steps. Solve by force. That is when you hold steady. That is when you say, we already have a system for this. And you walk them through how the team is already solving the problem with discipline.

You will know the case landed when the conversation shifts from what Lean costs to what it protects. When people stop asking why we still do it and start asking how to use it for the next issue.

Lean has to earn its place. Not just once. But every time the context shifts. That is not failure. That is the work. You lead it by staying calm, staying present, and staying anchored in results. Not in slides. In action. In impact. In proof. Every time. That is how you keep it real. That is how you keep it going.

The Research Behind It

Research from McKinsey shows that most Lean transformations stall not from poor execution but from shifting priorities. Their global operations study found that when a new business pressure emerged, like a merger, a budget cut, or a strategic pivot, Lean was one of the first systems to lose attention unless it was already built into decision making.

The mistake was not ignoring Lean. The mistake was thinking Lean was something extra. Something separate.

The Lean Enterprise Institute published case studies showing the same pattern. In organizations where Lean was seen as a separate initiative, it had to be resold every time a new leader came in or a new challenge appeared. But in places where Lean was positioned as the method for solving problems and improving delivery, it stayed intact. Even when the business changed, Lean was not pushed aside. It was used.

Amy Edmondson's research on team dynamics adds depth to this. When the environment shifts, people look for what feels safe and proven. If Lean is linked to solving the last major challenge, they stick with it. If Lean was just something tied to a single initiative or person, they step away. The perception of relevance is what holds the system.

John Shook, one of the original Lean practitioners at Toyota, wrote that Lean is only sustainable when it is viewed as the best way to solve business problems, not as a philosophy to protect. That means the system must re-earn its relevance as the business shifts. That is not a weakness. That is the strength of a practical system. It adapts. But only if leaders bring it forward.

The research is clear. Lean does not fade because it stops working. It fades when it stops being visible during moments that matter. When the pressure shows up, the system either proves its value or gets replaced by noise. Your job is to make sure it proves its value. Not with speeches. With facts. With behavior. With action that shows Lean still solves what matters.

That is what keeps Lean in the room. That is what keeps it real. And that is what leaders have to do. Not once. Every time the ground shifts. Quiet. Steady. Focused. That is how Lean holds up under change. And that is how you lead it forward.

Finish Strong So the System Is Not Forgotten

Most Lean efforts fade at the finish line. A change gets made. A problem gets solved. And then nothing. No closeout. No reflection. No reset. The team moves on. The board goes quiet. And the habit weakens. Not because people do not care. Because no one anchored the improvement.

The end of a problem is not the end of the work. It is the moment to lock in what was learned. You write the new standard. You update the visuals. You coach what to keep doing. That is how Lean holds. Not with effort. With follow through.

When a fix works, document the steps. Nothing fancy. A checklist. A quick summary. What changed. Why it mattered. What it looks like now. That becomes the new baseline. Without it, the next person guesses. And the improvement slips.

Review the change with the team. Ask what was learned. Ask what should be added to training. Ask if anything still needs to be adjusted. That reflection is not extra. It is what makes the improvement last. You are not finishing the project. You are anchoring the behavior.

You will know this is working when the team closes out their own work without being told. When they bring back what they learned. When the new way holds without reminders. That is the sign the system is strong.

> Lean is not a rush to the next thing. It is the discipline to protect what already works. And that discipline shows up in how you finish. If you skip the end, the next effort starts weaker. If you finish well, the next one starts stronger. That is how Lean grows. Not just by solving. By sticking. Finish the work. Lock the gain. Move forward with clarity. That is what leaders do. That is what makes Lean last.

The Research Behind It

Studies from the Lean Enterprise Institute show that one of the most common failure points in Lean systems is the failure to close out improvements. When a change is made but not documented, reinforced, or reflected on, it creates what they call a "shallow gain." It looks like progress. But it does not last. The fix fades. The habit weakens. The next improvement starts on uneven ground.

James Womack and Daniel Jones have written that sustained systems follow a simple pattern. Problem. Fix. Lock. Repeat. Without the lock, the process resets every time someone changes roles or priorities shift. That weakens the system. That creates rework. Their follow-up studies found that strong teams spent as much time anchoring the improvement as they did making it.

Toyota's internal practices reinforce this. After every change, they do not just move on. They review what changed. They write a new standard. They coach it. They adjust visuals. They reflect as a team. That is not extra. That is how they protect the system from slipping. The routine is clear. Finish the fix. Make it visible. Teach it. That is what holds the gain.

John Kotter's research on change management includes the same principle. He found that many organizations create change, but few sustain it. One reason is that the change is never institutionalized. People know something improved. But they do not know how or why. So the next person guesses. Or worse, undoes it. His conclusion was simple. If you want a change to last, you have to finish it. And then make it part of how the work runs.

James Clear, in his work on behavior and habits, points out that systems that stick are systems that are closed. Open loops drain attention. They create noise. Closed loops free up energy. When a team knows the change was finalized and the expectation is clear, they stop guessing. They start owning.

The research is clear. A fix without follow through is a temporary win. It looks good. But it does not hold. Strong systems finish what they start. They lock the gain. They coach the habit. They protect the progress. Not once. Every time. That is what builds momentum. That is what sustains the culture. And that is what the best Lean leaders do without needing to be asked. Quiet. Consistent. Complete.

In Summary

Lean will be tested. Not once. Over and over. The pressure will show up. Priorities will shift. Leaders will change. Habits will drift. And doubt will creep in. That is not a surprise. That is the signal that something real is happening. The question is not if it will happen. The question is how you lead when it does.

This chapter has shown that resistance is not a barrier. It is a test. A test of presence. A test of belief. A test of whether the system was built to last or just built to launch. You do not beat resistance with louder speeches or tighter control. You beat it with steady behavior. With clarity. With discipline. With proof.

You lead through it by staying close to the work. By resetting habits before they slip too far. By anchoring what was learned so it does not fade. You do not just start the system. You protect it. You hold the rhythm when others let go. That is what real Lean leadership looks like. Quiet. Daily. Repeated.

Now that we have worked through the challenges, it is time to focus on the person leading through them. The next chapter is not about tools. It is about you. It is about what Lean leadership looks like when it is done right. The habits. The presence. The discipline that makes it stick. Not in theory. In how you show up. Every day. Let's get into what that takes. Let's get into what it means to lead with Lean. For real.

Chapter Sixteen

Lean Leader Behaviors

Lean leadership is not about personality. It is not about charisma, motivation, or how loud someone can say the right words in a meeting. It is about behavior. Quiet. Consistent. Repeated. In the moments that matter most. Anyone can talk about culture. But Lean leaders shape it by how they show up every day.

This chapter is not a checklist. It is not a job description. It is a mirror. Because the strength of a Lean system does not come from the tools. It comes from the people protecting the rhythm when the noise gets loud. That is the difference. Not what they know. What they do. Every day. Without being told.

Lean leaders do not wait to be convinced. They do not need a new initiative to start leading this way. They use boards because they help. They coach thinking because it builds strength. They ask questions because they care about what is actually happening, not just what is being said. The team does not need to be pushed. The work pulls them forward because the behavior around them sets the tone.

This chapter will walk through what that looks like in real terms. Not theory. Practice. What Lean leaders do to keep the system strong, even when pressure shows up. What they repeat until it becomes normal. What they protect even when no one is watching. This is not a style. It is a discipline. And it is what makes the difference between Lean being installed and Lean being lived.

Let's break it down. Behavior by behavior. Simple. Clear. No fluff. Just the work. Done right. By leaders who know how to keep Lean real.

Leads by example every day

Leaders do not build a Lean culture by what they say in a meeting. They build it by how they show up when no one is watching. The strongest signal in any system is behavior. If you want daily habits to hold, they have to start with the people at the top. This does not mean perfection. It means consistency. Leaders who walk the floor, ask real questions, join huddles, and support problem solving send a message that Lean is not a program. It is how the work is done.

Leading by example is not about visibility for show. It is about presence with purpose. It means showing up when the board looks rough, not just when it looks clean. It means asking about blockers, not just metrics. It means standing in the process, watching the flow, and asking what feels harder than it should. When teams see that kind of behavior often enough, they stop performing and start engaging. That is when the shift happens.

If you say problem solving matters but never slow down to coach it, the team sees the gap. If you expect standard work but never check if it is being followed, the standard weakens. If you skip huddles but expect the team to run them, the habit fades. Your presence is not just about being seen. It is about reinforcing the discipline. Quiet. Daily. Without exception.

You do not need a calendar full of Lean events. You need small moments, repeated often. One question asked at the right time. One problem surfaced without punishment. One improvement supported without waiting for a pitch. These are the things that show Lean is not optional. It is normal.

You will know this behavior is in place when people reference what you do, not what you said. When teams prepare for your visit not because they are worried, but because they expect engagement. When people follow the rhythm even when you are not in the room. That is the signal. That is the standard.

Leading by example is not a slogan. It is a habit. If you want Lean to last, show the team what it looks like. Every day. Without needing to be asked. That is the work. That is the weight. That is what earns trust. And that is what holds the culture.

Supports daily improvement at every level

Lean is not something that happens once a quarter in a workshop. It is something that happens every day in real work. Strong Lean leaders know this. They do not wait for the big initiative or the next event. They build a system where improvement is expected, supported, and owned by the people closest to the problem. That only happens when leaders treat daily improvement like part of the job, not a bonus when there is time.

Supporting daily improvement starts with how you respond. When a team brings up friction, do you listen? When someone tests a countermeasure, do you make space to learn from it? When a process gets better, do you recognize the effort? These moments are what shape the culture. If you only engage when the issue is big or the fix is perfect, people stop trying. But if you show up for the small stuff, they keep going. One blocker removed. One handoff clarified. One step made easier. That is how Lean grows.

This behavior also means removing the barriers that stop improvement. It means protecting time for teams to think. It means letting them test something without needing a slide deck. It means shifting the question from who approved this to what did we learn. Daily improvement dies under red tape. It thrives when leaders clear the path and back the effort.

> You do not need to lead the change. You need to support it. That means asking the right questions. What are we solving today? What did we try last time? What made the difference? These are not status updates. They are prompts that keep thinking sharp. When teams hear them often enough, they start asking them without you.

You will know you are supporting daily improvement when teams bring forward changes without waiting for a kickoff. When the visual board shows movement. When the fixes are simple, focused, and grounded in what actually helps. You will also know it is working when the conversation shifts from fixing what broke to asking what else can be made better.

Lean is not powered by events. It is powered by habits. The daily ones. The small ones. The ones you do not see on a chart but feel in the room. Support those, and the system holds. Stay close to that rhythm, and the team will keep moving. That is what leadership looks like. Not in big moves. In daily action. Quiet. Steady. Always moving forward.

Stays present in the work

Lean leaders do not lead from a distance. They stay in the work. They go where the value is created. They see it for themselves. Not just when there is a problem. Not just during a review. Every week. Every cycle. Not because they are checking up. Because they are staying connected.

This presence is not about control. It is about clarity. When you watch the work unfold in real time, you learn what is really happening. You see where the friction lives. You hear how the team talks about the process. You spot what is missing before it turns into something bigger. That is the kind of visibility reports cannot give you. And it is the kind of leadership the team feels.

Staying present means showing up with purpose. You are not there to fix. You are there to see. You ask questions. You walk the process. You stand quietly and take in the flow. Then you ask what is making it harder than it needs to be. And you listen. That rhythm builds trust. When people see that you are willing to step into their space with respect and curiosity, they open up. They stop performing. They start telling you the truth.

The best Lean leaders have a routine. They block time to go see. They keep a notebook. They follow up. They do not show up to audit. They show up to learn. And when they do, the culture holds. Because the people doing the work know the person leading it is not guessing. They are watching. They are walking. They are staying present.

You will know this behavior is working when the team does not flinch when you show up. When they point out what is wrong instead of hiding it. When they ask you to walk the process with them. That is the shift. That is when presence becomes normal. That is when it becomes part of the system.

Lean does not survive without presence. The further leadership gets from the work, the faster the culture drifts. Staying close is not about catching mistakes. It is about keeping the work real. Keeping it grounded. And keeping yourself connected to what matters. That is how Lean stays alive. One visit at a time. Repeated. Without drama. With purpose. Every time.

Builds capability instead of dependency

Lean leaders do not make themselves the answer. They build teams that can think, act, and improve without waiting to be told. This is not about stepping back. It is about stepping in with the right questions. You coach instead of control. You shape the thinking without taking over the action.

The mistake many leaders make is trying to be helpful by solving everything. They jump in. They fix. They give advice before the team has a chance to work through the problem. It feels faster. It looks supportive. But it creates dependence. And dependence is what weakens systems. When the team learns that only the leader has the solution, they stop looking for it themselves. That is not strength. That is fragility.

Lean leaders ask instead of answer. They slow the moment down. They use five simple questions. What is the problem? What is causing it? What have you tried? What happened? What will you do next? These are not scripts. They are habits. They help the team think. They help the leader stay focused on building skill, not just fixing issues.

> Building capability means making time to reflect. It means letting the team struggle a little. Not so much that they stall. Just enough that they grow. You stay present. You offer support. But you do not jump to the fix. You give them the tools. You give them the structure. You give them the space to learn by doing.

You will know this is working when the team starts solving problems before you ask. When they bring options, not complaints. When they talk about process, not just pressure. That is capability. That is ownership. That is a system that gets stronger every time someone faces a challenge and knows what to do.

Dependency looks like speed. Capability is what creates scale. Lean leaders know the difference. They are not in the room to be the smartest. They are in the room to build more people who can lead the work without them. That is what makes the system grow. That is what keeps it alive. Not just today. Long after the leader moves on.

Stays grounded in the actual work

Lean leaders do not lead from the report. They lead from the floor. They do not assume the system is running because the metrics say so. They go see it. They listen. They watch. They learn. The truth of the work lives in the details most people skip. And Lean leaders never skip the details.

This behavior matters because every system looks cleaner on paper. Boards get updated. Dashboards glow green. But the real signals show up in the flow, in the conversations, in the small moments where the process either holds or breaks. If a leader is not present for those moments, they start leading from distance. And distance dulls their judgment.

> Staying grounded does not mean micromanaging. It means showing up with purpose. You ask questions. You watch how work is triggered. You listen for where people hesitate or struggle. You are not there to audit. You are there to understand. And that understanding gives your decisions weight.

When a team sees their leader show up, not just when something goes wrong, but because they want to know what is real, that sends a signal. It tells people that the process matters. It tells them that small gaps will not be ignored. It tells them that leadership is not just about alignment. It is about awareness.

You will know this behavior is strong when your presence stops being a performance trigger. When the team talks to you like they talk to each other. When they show you what is hard, not just what is done. That is when you know they trust you. That is when you know your insight is grounded.

Go see is not a Lean tool. It is a leadership standard. If you are not willing to walk the floor, you are not ready to lead the system. Lean happens in real places, through real people, solving real problems. And the only way to lead that is to be in it. Not once. Not for show. But often. Quietly. With curiosity. That is how you stay grounded. That is how you earn the right to lead the work.

Protects the habits that make the system work

Lean only lasts when the habits behind it hold. The boards. The huddles. The coaching. The problem solving. These are not optional extras. They are the operating rhythm. The moment they slip, the system starts to slide. And it does not matter what the strategy says, if the daily habits fade, Lean goes with them.

Lean leaders know this. So they protect the habits. Not with pressure. With presence. They show up to huddles on time. They ask questions that reinforce thinking. They expect boards to be updated because the board is how the work stays visible. They do not wait for a performance dip to pay attention. They use the habits to prevent the dip in the first place.

This is not about being rigid. It is about being reliable. People do not trust a system that changes every time the pressure goes up. If the huddle only happens when the calendar allows, or if the problem solving only runs when someone important is watching, the culture becomes compliance. That is how Lean fades.

But when leaders treat the habits as nonnegotiable, not because of a rule, but because of what they enable, the team learns to do the same. The habits become routine. The routines build rhythm. And the rhythm gives the system its strength.

You will know this behavior is working when the habits hold even when you are not in the room. When the huddle runs without a prompt. When the board reflects real blockers, not just status. When the team brings problems forward and starts solving before they are asked. That is the signal that the system is not just active. It is owned.

Protecting habits does not require a speech. It requires repetition. It requires showing people, every day, that these small routines are not just tools, they are how the work stays real. They are how the team stays focused. They are how the culture stays intact when everything else starts to shift. That is what Lean leaders do. Quiet. Steady. Committed to the habits because they know that is what holds the system together.

Leader Reflection: Are You Leading Lean or Watching It?

Take ten quiet minutes. No email. No slides. Just you and these questions. You are not scoring yourself. You are holding up a mirror. Because Lean does not rise on strategy. It rises on behavior. And your behavior sets the tone.

1. Do your actions match what you say Lean is?

Think about the last week. Did you coach in the moment or just comment after the fact? Did you attend the huddle with purpose or just show up to be seen? When you walked past the board, did you ask about blockers or just glance and keep moving? If someone shadowed you for a day, would they see Lean in how you lead, or just in what you say?

2. Do you show up consistently or when convenient?

Lean is not something you do when you have time. It is something you make time for. What happens to your routines when pressure shows up? Do the huddles hold? Do the conversations stay focused? Or do they quietly disappear until the next review? Your consistency is the culture's foundation. When it cracks, the system does too.

3. *Do you solve problems or create the space for others to?*

Think back to the last problem raised in your team. Did you offer a fix right away? Or did you pause, ask questions, and let the team take the lead? Your instinct matters here. If your first move is to solve, the team learns to wait. If your first move is to ask, they learn to think. That is the difference between compliance and ownership.

4. *Do you reinforce the right behavior or just react to results?*

When the numbers move, do you ask what changed or just celebrate the win? When the metrics dip, do you ask about learning or just apply pressure? Results matter. But how they are achieved matters more. If your response is only tied to outcomes, the team learns to manage perception instead of improving process. That is when the culture starts to slide.

5. *Do you coach people through the hard parts or just check progress?*

The team does not need more oversight. They need more support. When they are stuck, when something slips, when an idea fails, are you the person who helps them reset, or the person they try to avoid? Your response in these moments either builds trust or erodes it. There is no neutral.

6. *Are you willing to hear the truth?*

When someone disagrees with you, do they feel safe saying it? When something is broken, do people speak up or stay quiet until you leave? Lean only works in truth. And truth only lives where leaders are willing to hear it without judgment. If your presence quiets the room, the system is already slipping.

> **Now choose one.** Pick the question that hit hardest. Not to feel bad. To get better. Write down what you will do differently this week. Maybe it is one habit you will protect more firmly. One question you will start asking in every huddle. One fix you will let the team own without stepping in. Keep it simple. Then do it. Not once. Every day. Without needing to be reminded.

Because Lean is not what you say. It is what you model. It is what the team sees. It is what gets repeated when you are not in the room. That is your impact. That is the real work. Quiet. Present. Honest. Consistent. One behavior at a time. That is how you lead Lean. And that is how it sticks.

In Summary

Lean does not hold because it was launched well. It holds because it is led well. Not in sprints. Not in special projects. Every day. Quiet. Present. Disciplined. The behaviors in this chapter are not theories. They are the foundation. They are what the best Lean leaders do when no one is watching. They ask questions that move the team forward. They model the habits they expect from others. They protect the system without needing to control it. And they lead through action, not announcements.

If you want your Lean system to last, stop asking if people believe in it. Start asking what you are doing to make it real. What you show up for. What you ignore. What you coach. What you repeat. That is what shapes the culture. That is what sets the tone. The tools do not create belief. The leadership does. And when that leadership is steady, the system has a chance to grow into something that lasts.

This is not about perfection. It is about presence. This is not about rollout. It is about rhythm. If you want to build a team that solves problems, adapts to change, and keeps getting better long after the spotlight moves on, it starts with how you lead. Every habit you model. Every conversation you choose to have. Every small action that reinforces the work.

We are almost there. One chapter left. Not about tools. Not about systems. About you. A call to lead with Lean. Not because it is easy. Because it is right. Because the work deserves it. Because the people do. Let's finish this strong. Let's talk about what it means to lead for real. Let's go.

Chapter Seventeen

A Call to Lead with Lean

Let's bring it home. This is not the end of the book. It is the start of the work.

Lean is not something you learn and then carry around like a credential. It is something you practice. It is something you live. And the way you lead either brings it to life or buries it under noise. You have seen the tools. You have walked through the habits. You have read the stories. Now it comes down to what happens next. Not in theory. In behavior.

The final chapter is not about information. It is about decision. It is a moment for leaders to pause, to get honest, and to ask themselves what kind of leadership they are willing to offer. Not someday. Right now. Because everything Lean promises, clarity, dignity, focus, and improvement, only shows up when someone chooses to lead in a way that earns it.

These next few sections are not about what to know. They are about who you are becoming. They are about what it takes to stay steady when the system is tested. They are about how real leadership is not always loud, but it is always present. Always clear. Always anchored.

It starts with one choice. One commitment. One moment where a leader decides that they will not just talk about Lean. They will lead with it.

Let's get into that moment. Let's name what it means. And then let's close strong. Because Lean does not live in what you say. It lives in what you do next.

Own the Choice

You do not become a Lean leader by accident. It is not a title. It is not a role you are assigned. It is a decision. Quiet. Repeated. Backed by what you do when no one is watching. You either choose to lead this way or you do not. And the longer you hesitate, the louder your actions speak.

Owning the choice means owning the impact you have. You are not neutral. You are setting the tone with every question you ask, every habit you protect, every routine you reinforce or let slide. If the team sees you show up for Lean only when it is convenient, they will treat it the same way. If they see you ask better questions, coach through the hard parts, and keep the rhythm steady, they will follow that lead.

This is not about saying you support Lean. It is about making decisions that prove it. Do you walk the board? Do you join the huddle? Do you slow down enough to coach a real problem instead of giving an answer? Do you keep the habits going when no one else is pushing? That is the test. That is the choice.

You will know you are leading with Lean when your behavior shows up in the team. When they start solving problems without waiting. When they speak up early instead of holding back. When they trust the system because they trust you to hold it steady.

> You cannot fake this. You either show up or you do not. And the system follows. Not because you said the right thing. Because you did the hard thing. Every day. Quiet. Present. Steady. That is the choice. And once you own it, everything else starts to move.

The Research Behind It

The theory behind owning the choice to lead with Lean draws from a blend of behavioral science, organizational psychology, and core principles of continuous improvement. At its heart is the idea that leadership behavior creates the culture, not the other way around. When leaders choose to engage consistently in Lean habits, those actions form the standard the rest of the organization responds to.

Albert Bandura's *Social Learning Theory* explains how people learn behaviors by observing others. In a Lean system, the leader is always being watched. Every time they coach a problem instead of fix it, every time they walk a board instead of ask for a report, they are reinforcing expectations. Bandura's research shows that consistent behavior from authority figures does not just model action. It creates belief.

Edgar Schein, a leading scholar in organizational culture, wrote that leaders embed culture through what they systematically pay attention to, measure, and react to. If a leader talks about Lean but does not participate in the daily huddle, the team will believe the huddle is optional. If the leader reinforces process thinking, problem solving, and clarity of work, that becomes the norm. Schein's work emphasizes that these signals are not accidental. They form the backbone of what the team perceives as real.

From a Lean standpoint, Womack and Jones consistently argued that the success of Lean has less to do with the tools and more to do with leadership commitment to a way of thinking and acting. They noted that Lean fails not because the system lacks potential, but because leadership fails to carry the behavior forward when the spotlight fades.

Jim Collins, in *Good to Great*, echoes this idea with his Level 5 Leadership framework. The most effective leaders do not rely on charisma or pressure. They create transformation through quiet discipline, consistency, and deep personal ownership. They choose to lead differently, and that decision changes the entire trajectory of the organization.

The theory is clear. Leadership choice creates system behavior. Repeated action creates culture. Presence beats slogans. If you want Lean to hold, the leader must choose to live it first. Not once. Not during the launch. But every day, especially when it is hard. That is not a leadership style. That is a system built on ownership. And it works.

Choose the Hard Thing on Purpose

Leading with Lean will eventually ask more of you than most systems do. Not because it is complex. Because it is clear. Lean shows where the gaps live. It makes visible what has been tolerated. It removes the option to look away. And that means, at some point, you will face a choice. Let it slide, or step in. Stay quiet, or ask the hard question. Move on, or fix what keeps breaking. These are not technical decisions. They are leadership decisions. And the best Lean leaders choose the hard thing on purpose.

Doing the hard thing is not about volume. It is not about intensity. It is about showing up when it matters. When the room is tired. When the routine slips. When someone says, we already tried. That is when your behavior sets the tone. Do you pull back and wait for a better time, or do you step forward and reset the standard. Not with pressure. With clarity. With presence. With the kind of steadiness that tells the team this is not optional. This is who we are.

> Choosing the hard thing also means not chasing the quick win. It means asking what is causing the problem instead of fixing the surface. It means holding the line when a new priority shows up. It means saying, this matters, even when the result is not visible yet. That kind of leadership does not shout. It holds steady. It stays real. It repeats the right behavior until the system follows.

You do not need to choose the hard thing every time. But you need to choose it often enough that people start to trust the pattern. They see that you are not just there when it is easy. You are there when it counts. And that is what makes Lean believable. Not because of the words. Because of the weight you carry when others pause.

Next, we will turn toward something just as important, learning how to pass that belief on. Leading with Lean is not just about what you do. It is about what you leave behind. That is where we go next. Let's talk about how to leave a mark that lasts.

Leave a Mark That Outlasts Your Role

The real test of leadership is not what happens while you are in the role. It is what happens after you are gone. If everything you built disappears when the nameplate changes, you led with influence, not with impact. Leading with Lean means leaving a system that holds without needing to be pushed. A rhythm that continues without being watched. A culture that keeps improving without asking for permission. That is the mark. That is what lasts.

Leaving a mark is not about personal credit. It is about shared ownership. When the team runs the huddle without you, when the board gets updated without a reminder, when the problems are raised and solved without escalation, that is the sign your leadership took root. You made the work better, but you also made the people better. That is how you know it will hold.

This only happens when leaders stop trying to control everything and start building systems others can run. You teach. You coach. You support. And slowly, the team does not need your presence to stay on track. They move the work forward because they believe in the method, not because they are trying to meet your standard. That is the shift. That is what creates durability.

You do not leave a mark by trying to be remembered. You leave it by helping others become strong enough that they do not need you anymore. The process keeps improving. The culture stays focused. The system grows. Not because you are still in the room. Because your leadership changed how the room works.

And that brings us to the final piece. The call to lead with Lean is not just about practice. It is about belief. It is about choosing to lead in a way that serves others, respects the work, and brings the best out of people even when no one is watching. Let's close with that call. Not to end the book. To begin the work. For real. For good. Let's finish strong.

The Research Behind It

Leadership impact is not measured by how much attention a person commands in the moment. It is measured by how well the system performs after that person is gone. Research across organizational psychology and operational excellence confirms this. In studies by the Center for Creative Leadership, long term team performance was tied more closely to leadership continuity of habits than to individual presence. Teams that sustained key routines, daily huddles, structured coaching, and problem solving cadence, retained performance gains regardless of turnover. Teams without those habits saw rapid regression once a leader left.

The Lean Enterprise Institute echoes this in its case studies. Organizations that treated Lean as leader driven initiatives saw temporary gains tied to personalities. When those leaders moved on, so did the energy. But where Lean was built into how the team worked every day, the impact remained. The habit was the anchor not the person.

James Womack has written that true Lean leadership is invisible. It is not about the person. It is about the pattern. The best leaders, he noted, left systems that worked better after they left. Because they did not center themselves. They built teams and systems that were stronger than any one name.

John Kotter's work on transformational change also supports this. In his follow up studies, change efforts that sustained for years were not the ones with the loudest launch. They were the ones with distributed ownership, daily habits, and clear expectations. Those patterns survived turnover because they were not tied to personality. They were tied to purpose.

The theory is simple and consistent. A leader who leaves a system stronger than they found it leads with humility and intent. The structure holds. The rhythm continues.

The improvement does not fade. Not because of speeches. Because of habits. That is the measure of impact. That is what makes leadership last. And that is the final call to lead in a way that leaves something better behind. Not for credit. For good.

Step In When It Matters Most

This is the part of leadership that cannot be delegated. There are moments when Lean is questioned. When something breaks. When pressure hits. When people look up. In those moments, the leader either proves the system matters or shows that it was optional all along. This is not about always having the answer. It is about showing up when it counts.

Every Lean system has a breaking point. The board does not get updated. A huddle gets skipped. A new leader wants to move faster. Someone pushes for results without asking about the process. That is when the culture is decided. Not in the smooth cycles. In the ones that test your discipline.

> Leaders who step in do not panic. They do not blame. They go back to basics. They walk the board. They ask about blockers. They reset the huddle. They coach the five whys. Not in a loud way. In a real way. Their presence says Lean still matters. Even now. Especially now.

This behavior is not about control. It is about rhythm. It is about keeping the system honest when the pressure invites shortcuts. When the team is tired. When leadership changes. When something urgent pulls attention away. That is when you step in, not to take over, but to hold the line.

You will know this behavior is present when the team does not freeze during tough moments. When they look for the board instead of avoiding it. When the process holds under pressure. That is not luck. That is leadership doing what it is supposed to do. Quiet. Steady. On time.

Great leaders do not show up to impress. They show up to anchor. To keep Lean from slipping into theory. To protect the behaviors that carry the system. They know exactly when to step in. And when they do, everything holds just a little stronger. That is not drama. That is discipline. That is how Lean stays alive.

The Research Behind It

The theory behind stepping in when it matters most is grounded in behavioral reinforcement and the psychology of cultural stability. Systems theory tells us that processes will drift unless they are monitored and corrected in real time. This is not micromanagement. This is system maintenance. When the environment changes or the stress rises, people will naturally revert to old behaviors unless the new ones are visibly reinforced. That reinforcement comes from leadership presence.

Edgar Schein's work on organizational culture explains that people watch what leaders do under pressure. Those moments set the tone. If a leader skips the huddle or walks past the visual board when performance slips, the team learns that the process does not matter under stress. If the leader shows up anyway asks questions, stays calm, and holds the rhythm, the team learns that Lean is not a preference. It is a standard.

This connects to Amy Edmondson's research on psychological safety. Teams will only speak up or surface issues when they believe it is safe and worth it. That belief is tested most when something goes wrong. If a leader steps in with curiosity and stability rather than control or blame, the system gains credibility. If they disappear, the team reverts to survival mode and the culture retreats.

James Clear's work on habit formation adds one more layer. Habits form through repetition and are held in place by cues and reinforcement. In Lean, those cues are things like huddles, boards, and structured check-ins. But the reinforcement comes from leaders. When the leader shows up for the routine even when it is tough, the habit strengthens. When the leader skips it, the habit erodes. One small absence sends a loud message.

Toyota's practice reinforces all of this. They do not wait until things go wrong to observe. They go see. They ask questions. They stay grounded in the work. That is how their leaders earn the right to lead change, not with vision decks, but with presence when it counts. That kind of consistency under stress is what makes Lean more than a toolkit. It makes it the way the organization actually works.

So the theory is clear. Systems hold when leaders reinforce the behavior during moments of pressure. It is not the plan that sustains the culture. It is the presence. Not loud. Not flashy. Just grounded. Timely. Real. That is what makes Lean resilient. And that is what great leaders bring.

In Summary

Lean does not need more theory. It needs more leaders who show up for it when it counts. This chapter has not been about knowledge. It has been about behavior. About the daily choices leaders make to keep Lean from becoming another forgotten initiative. When leaders show up with consistency, when they protect the habits, when they step in at the right moments and stay quiet at the right times, they turn Lean from a system into a standard.

This is not about being perfect. It is about being present. Culture does not hold because of what is written on the wall. It holds because of how leaders show up when the room gets loud, when the path gets unclear, and when the team needs something solid to anchor to. That is the work. That is the role. That is the call.

The next chapter is not about tools or behaviors. It is about the decision that comes after all of it. The decision to lead with Lean. Not just run Lean events. Not just talk about Lean values. But to choose it, every day, even when no one is asking for it. Even when it would be easier to let it fade. The final chapter is a call to that kind of leadership. Not louder. Not newer. Just real. Let's close the book by asking the only question that matters now: What kind of leader will you choose to be?

Chapter Eighteen

Wrapping Up

This book was not written to inspire. It was written to anchor. To remind leaders that Lean is not about fanfare. It is about discipline. It is about presence. It is about what happens every day in real work, with real teams, under real pressure. If you were looking for a playbook, you already saw it. If you were looking for a script, you *missed the point*. This was never about having the perfect words. It was about having the steady habits.

> Lean works when leaders lead it. Not with energy. With clarity. Not with complexity. With rhythm. Not by doing everything. By doing what matters and doing it often enough that the culture starts to hold. You do not need a big rollout to lead this way. You need a decision. Quiet. Clear. Backed by behavior. Every time. That is what makes Lean stick.

You read about the tools. You studied the habits. You heard from other leaders who made it real. Not because they had extra time. Because they led with purpose. And they kept leading through resistance, doubt, turnover, pressure, and drift. You saw what it looks like to stay steady when the habits start slipping. You saw how belief is built through repetition. Not through a speech. Through a system that holds up under change. That is what makes it work. That is what makes it last.

And now we are here. The last page. The last line. But not the end. This is the start. Because the only thing that matters now is what you do next. Not what you say. Not what you plan. What you do. When no one is watching. When the pressure is high. When the spotlight moves on. That is the test. That is the call.

You do not have to lead Lean perfectly. But you have to lead it on purpose. You have to show up when it would be easier to step back. You have to coach when it would be faster to fix. You have to protect the rhythm when everyone else is drifting. That is leadership. That is the work.

So take a breath. Look around. Then decide. Are you going to be the kind of leader who waits for belief? Or the kind who earns it. One habit at a time. One team at a time. One decision at a time.

Not someday. Right now.

Let's go.

Lean Leader Glossary

Here is a list of common terms found in this book as well as in Lean organizations.

5 Whys

A simple but powerful root cause analysis tool where you ask "why" five times to uncover the underlying reason a problem is occurring. The value is in the thinking, not the number.

A3

A structured problem-solving template (often one page in length) used to document the Define-Measure-Analyze-Improve-Control (DMAIC)-like process of continuous improvement in a simple, visual format.

Andon

A visual signaling system that alerts teams or leaders to problems in real time so immediate action can be taken. Originally used in factories, now adapted for service and digital environments.

Batching

Processing multiple items at once instead of one at a time. While sometimes efficient, batching often introduces delays and hides defects, making flow less visible and response slower.

Catchball

A back-and-forth exchange between leaders and teams to test and refine ideas collaboratively. It ensures alignment and feedback before implementation.

Cycle Time

The total time it takes to complete one unit of work, from start to finish. Used to identify efficiency and potential delays.

Daily Management

A discipline of holding short, regular check-ins to discuss problems, progress, and priorities. Keeps teams aligned and accountable.

Flow

The smooth, continuous movement of work through a process without delays, bottlenecks, or rework. Central to Lean thinking.

Gemba

A Japanese term meaning "the real place" or where the work happens. Lean leaders are expected to "go to the gemba" to see problems firsthand rather than relying on reports.

Handoff

The transfer of responsibility or information from one person or team to another. Often a source of delay or error if not done well.

Jidoka

A Lean principle that empowers anyone to stop the process when a defect is found. Focuses on building quality into the process rather than inspecting for it later.

Just-in-Time (JIT)

A production and workflow method that focuses on delivering exactly what is needed, when it is needed, and in the amount needed to minimize waste.

Kanban

A visual scheduling system that uses cards or digital signals to track work in progress. Helps limit work in process (WIP) and improves flow.

Lead Time

The total elapsed time from the moment a request is made until it is fulfilled. Includes both value-added and non-value-added time.

Lean

A philosophy and set of tools focused on eliminating waste, increasing value, and empowering people to solve real problems in real time.

Leader Standard Work

The set of repeatable daily, weekly, and monthly behaviors that guide how Lean leaders show up. Focuses on setting direction, supporting teams, and reinforcing problem-solving habits.

Pareto Chart

A bar graph that displays problems in order of frequency or impact. Helps teams focus on the few issues causing the most trouble (often based on the 80/20 rule).

PDCA (Plan-Do-Check-Act)

A scientific method for testing changes, reflecting on outcomes, and improving processes iteratively.

PCE (Process Cycle Efficiency)

A metric that measures how much of total process time is spent on value-added activity. Calculated as: (Value-added time / Total time) × 100%.

Root Cause

The underlying reason a problem occurs. Lean aims to address root causes instead of symptoms.

Spaghetti Diagram

A tool used to map the actual movement of people or materials through a space. The "spaghetti" lines show inefficiencies and unnecessary motion.

Standard Work

A documented and agreed-upon way of doing something. It serves as a baseline for training, improvement, and recovery during change.

Takt Time

The rate at which work needs to be completed to meet customer demand. Calculated as available time divided by customer demand. Keeps teams aligned to flow rather than speed.

Visual Management

Using visible indicators like boards, charts, or color cues to make status, issues, and priorities easy to see and act on.

Voice of the Customer (VOC)

The expressed and unexpressed needs, expectations, and feedback from those the process serves. A guide for prioritizing improvement.

Waste (Muda)

Any activity that does not add value for the customer. Lean identifies eight categories of waste: defects, overproduction, waiting, non-utilized talent, transportation, inventory, motion, and extra processing.

Work in Process (WIP)

Items that have been started but are not yet complete. High WIP can indicate bottlenecks and reduces visibility into flow.

Crafting a Problem Statement

The problem statement is where clarity begins. It forces the team to slow down just long enough to agree on what is actually broken before rushing to fix it. Done well, it becomes a compass. Not just for the solution, but for the effort, the energy, and the attention that follows. Here's how to do it right.

The Four Core Elements

- **Be Clear and Concise**

    Say what's broken in plain language. No jargon. No filler. People should nod when they hear it, not ask for a translation.

- **Highlight the Impact**

    What is this costing us? Time, money, trust, morale? Make it obvious why this is worth solving. Otherwise, it will slide off the radar.

- **Define the Scope**

    Set boundaries. What part of the process are we talking about? What is included, and just as important, what is not?

- **Get Feedback from the SMEs**

    Subject matter experts know where the pain is real and where it's just noise. Bring them in early. Not to approve, but to inform.

A Strong Problem Statement Aligns and Drives

- It brings stakeholders into focus.
- It prevents teams from solving the wrong thing.
- It directs energy toward solutions that actually matter.
- It keeps the customer's need at the center.

Team-Based Steps for Success

1. Gather a small group of SMEs. Keep it focused. Keep it grounded.
2. Walk through these questions and answer them collaboratively
    - What is the problem that needs solved?
    - Why is it a problem?
    - Where is the problem observed?
    - Who is impacted?
    - When was it first observed?
    - How is it observed (symptoms)?
    - How often does it happen?
    - What data is needed to quantify it?
3. Collect the data
    Data grounds urgency. It turns gut feeling into proof.
4. Quantify the impact
    Show how big the pain is. Make the case.
5. Write the statement
    With the team. With the facts. In plain terms. An easy format for your statement

is:

> Since (How long this has been a problem), (What is the problem you are trying to solve. As a result, (The listed, quantified impacts of having the problem).

Bottom Line

Do not problem solve in a vacuum. The quality of the solution depends on how clearly the problem is understood. Get it right on page one, and the rest moves faster, with less confusion, fewer detours, and stronger buy-in.

Standard Work for Leaders Cheat Sheet

Leadership needs rhythm. Not to control people, but to stay connected to the work, the team, and the truth. Standard work is how leaders keep Lean alive after the excitement fades. It is not a checklist. It is a set of anchors that ensure the right behaviors keep showing up, even when the pressure is on.

These templates are not rigid. They are reminders. Small prompts that keep the thinking sharp and the actions honest.

Daily Gemba Walk Template

- **Purpose**: Stay visible. Listen without filtering. Spot the drift early.
- **Time**: 15–30 minutes
- **Focus**: Go see, ask why, show respect

What to Look For

- Is the visual management current and used?
- Are teams clear on today's priorities?
- Are blockers visible and being addressed?
- Are people solving problems or working around them?

What to Ask

- "What's working today?"
- "What's slowing us down?"
- "What support do you need from me?"

Weekly Reflection with Direct Reports

- **Purpose**: Reflect. Refocus. Recommit.
- **Time**: 30–60 minutes

What to Cover

- What problems did we surface and solve this week?
- Where did we get stuck?
- What are we learning?
- What needs my help?

> Mini-prompt: "Show me the change, not the slide"

Monthly Check-In on System Health

- **Purpose**: Zoom out. Spot patterns. Adjust approach.
- **Time**: 60 minutes

Review Together

- Are KPIs holding or drifting?
- Are huddles routine or meaningful?
- Where is standard work slipping?
- What part of the system needs reinforcement?

> Mini-prompt: "Where is the noise drowning out the signal?"

Quarterly Team Reset

- **Purpose**: Reground the team. Clarify the mission. Reignite energy.
- **Time**: Half-day

Discuss Openly

- What wins are we proud of?
- Where have we gone off track?
- What habits do we need to rebuild?
- What's next that matters?

> Mini-prompt: "What do we need to stop pretending is working?"

Bottom Line

Standard work for leaders is not about control. It is about consistency. You are not there to micromanage. You are there to make sure Lean does not become theater. These touchpoints are how leaders keep the habits real, the focus sharp, and the culture honest. The goal is not to complete a form. It is to be the kind of leader the system needs, steady, curious, and present.